APPLIED
RESEARCH
METHODS FOR

MASS
COMMUNICATORS

OTHER BOOKS OF INTEREST FROM
MARQUETTE BOOKS

Jami A. Fullerton and Alice G. Kendrick, *Advertising's War on Terrorism: The Story of the U.S. State Department's Shared Values Initiative Program* (2006). ISBN: 0-922993-43-2 (cloth); 0-922993-44-0 (paperback)

Stephen D. Cooper, *Watching the Watchdog: Bloggers as the Fifth Estate* (2006). ISBN: 0-922993-46-7 (cloth); 0-922993-47-5 (paperback)

Mitch Land and Bill Hornaday (editors), *Contemporary Media Ethics: A Practical Guide for Students, Scholars and Professionals* (2006). ISBN: 0-922993-41-6 (cloth); 0-922993-42-4 (paperback)

Ralph D. Berenger (ed.), *Cybermedia Go to War: Role of Alternative Media During the 2003 Iraq War* (2006). ISBN: 0-922993-24-6

David Demers, *Dictionary of Mass Communication: A Guide for Students, Scholars and Professionals* (2005). ISBN: 0-922993-35-1 (cloth); 0-922993-25-4 (paperback)

John Burke, *From Prairie to Palace: The Lost Biography of Buffalo Bill* (2005). Introduction by Dr. Jason Berger; edited by Tim Connor. ISBN: 0-922993-21-1

John C. Merrill, Ralph D. Berenger and Charles J. Merrill, *Media Musings: Interviews with Great Thinkers* (2004). ISBN: 0-922993-15-7

Ralph D. Berenger (ed.), *Global Media Go to War: Role of Entertainment and News During the 2003 Iraq War* (2004). ISBN: 0-922993-10-6

Melvin L. DeFleur and Margaret H. DeFleur, *Learning to Hate Americans: How U.S. Media Shape Negative Attitudes Among Teenagers in Twelve Countries* (2003). ISBN: 0-922993-05-X

David Demers (ed.), *Terrorism, Globalization and Mass Communication: Papers Presented at the 2002 Center for Global Media Studies Conference* (2003). ISBN: 0-922993-04-1

APPLIED
RESEARCH
METHODS FOR

MASS
COMMUNICATORS

JOEY REAGAN

MARQUETTE BOOKS
SPOKANE, WASHINGTON

Library of Congress Cataloging-in-Publication Data

Reagan, Joey.
    Applied research methods for mass communicators / Joey Reagan.
        p. cm.
    Includes bibliographical references and index.
    ISBN-13: 978-0-922993-45-1 (pbk. : alk. paper)
    ISBN-10: 0-922993-45-9 (pbk. : alk. paper)
        1. Mass media--Research--Methodology. I. Title.
    P91.3.R32 2006
    001.4--dc22

                                                                2006020422

MARQUETTE BOOKS
3107 E. 62nd Avenue
Spokane, WA 99223
509-443-7057 (phone)
509-448-2191 (fax)
books@marquettebooks.org
www.MarquetteBooks.org

TABLE OF CONTENTS

PREFACE

The purpose of this book is to help you understand the basics of research and to make you a more knowledgeable consumer of research. In fact, after reading this book and participating in an introductory research class, you should be able to conduct simple projects on your own or with just a little outside help.

There are many types of research projects you can do on your own. You can do informal research. You can carry out simple telephone surveys. You can set up and analyze basic databases and calculate percentages and averages in your spreadsheet. Knowing the jargon of research — which includes such terms as "mean," "median," "random," and "longitudinal study" — will help you understand reports and communicate with your research director or consultant. With this knowledge, those researchers also will lose their "priest-like" status.

Many of the concepts in this book also can be applied to work and life even if you are not conducting a research project. For example, a knowledge of random selection methods can help you make decisions about how to assign offices or select employees for tasks. You will have a better understanding of polls that are taken during an election season and of research that examines whether violent television content is affecting your child. With that knowledge, you can make better voting decisions or decide whether and how to control your child's TV viewing.

My assumption in writing this book is that you are most likely going to be a communication professional. You will be designing campaigns, managing accounts, selling advertising, and doing other communication tasks. You will evaluate the impact of promotions, make programming decisions or decide on the best style or layout. You will read research reports, apply results to your campaign, contract for research when you need to know who uses your products, discuss projects with your research department when you need to know your target, and respond to advertisers when they want to know the composition or purchase behavior of their audiences.

Both quantitative and qualitative methods are covered, but more time is spent on quantitative methods because so much of the research you will encounter is based on numbers, such as ratings and identifying target audiences and their behaviors. While de-emphasizing statistical calculations, I have included a few statistical tests as examples to illustrate how to interpret numbers that describe or form relations.

This book pays a lot of attention to variables. Several chapters are devoted to defining variables, operationalizing them, and evaluating their reliability and validity. You will ultimately have to answer questions like: Did my campaign (before vs. after) affect the image of my company? What subsets of the market are most likely to use my product? What characteristics (income, age, etc.) of the audience for my syndicated TV program are most valued by my advertisers? These questions are all about variables and relations.

This book is not meant to teach you ratings, media buying, and other skills that you will learn in other books and classes. It is designed to help you understand the research that produces those reports so that you can make judgments about the meaning of those reports and how well the research was done.

Notice that there is not one best way to do research. There are, of course, incompetent ways. But deciding how to collect data or whether to do a survey or focus group depends on your needs. Part of your job is also knowing which is appropriate: when to do research and when *not* to do research.

Keep in mind that research is only one of the tools that will help you make better decisions. The ultimate reason for reading this book is to help you make better decisions as a professional and citizen. If you were making a bet, which would you rather have, a fifty-fifty chance of winning or a 95% chance of winning? That's what research can do for you: increase the odds that you will make a correct decision.

ACKNOWLEDGMENTS

I appreciate permission from the following companies, organizations and people who have allowed me to use their work in this book or who provided grants for research through Washington State University (in alphabetical order):

American Association for Public Opinion Research
Anne Ellen's Cookies and Anne Schwartz

Erica Austin, Washington State University
Camp Fire USA, Central Puget Sound Council
Claritas Inc.
Janay Collins, Microsoft Corporation
Tom Greenbaum, Groups Plus, Inc.
International Association of Business Communicators
Kadlec Medical Center, Richland, Washington
Virginia McCarty, McCarty and Associates, Inc.
Nielsen Media Research
National Opinion Research Center, University of Chicago
Reagan Market Research
Recreational Equipment, Inc.
Red Robin International, Inc.
Scott Simms, Portland General Electric
Ching-Quo Wu

CHAPTER 1

WHY LEARN ABOUT RESEARCH?

Research directors and consultants who conduct polls, do ratings studies and carry out other projects must understand research methods and statistics to do their jobs. They must be experts. You might also assume that media sales people must understand research because they use ratings and other data to sell advertising. But it's not so obvious that other communication professionals need to understand research, too. For example, people who write public relations news releases must understand their audiences and the types of content and style that are most effective in reaching them. People who undertake creative projects also need research skills to evaluate the effectiveness of those projects or campaigns. This chapter points out that *all* communication professionals need to learn something about research to be successful in their jobs.

RESEARCH SKILLS ARE CRITICAL FOR YOUR JOB

A recent broadcast industry want-ad for a sales manager specified that applicants must have a "working knowledge of Scarborough, Nielsen Ratings." Another recent ad for an advertising account executive required an "in-depth knowledge of ratings, research and computer skills." An online ad for a strategic planning project manager stated that "exposure to market research tools and techniques is a definite plus."

Even mass communicators who work on the creative side need to know something about research. Take, for instance, the following want-ad for a broadcast news producer: "Experienced producer to lead our marquee newscasts. Organization and aggressive research skills are a must."

Public relations professionals can obtain accreditation through the Universal Accreditation Board (UAB). More than 75 percent of jobs posted in mid-2005 in the Public Relations Society of America job center specified UAB accreditation was "preferred." The UAB test requires analytical abilities, including "Objectively interprets data. Thinks logically. Identifies appropriate audiences (publics) and the concerns of each. Determines if goals and objectives of public relations program were met." And two sections of the test require research skills: "Develops a hypothesis. Develops the research plan. Determines appropriate qualitative and quantitative methods. Decides on the population and sampling techniques to use with that population. Designs instruments (questionnaire, interview, etc.). Uses the acceptable techniques to collect data. Codes and analyzes results and presents findings."

So you can see that many types of jobs in communication require fluency in research. Such knowledge will help you get a job and perform well once you are in it.

COMMUNICATION PROFESSIONALS SAY...

As a major tool of communication professionals, research can be applied to most aspects of decision making. Research helps you understand the image of your company, how people feel about campaign issues, public opinion, how the market works and many other aspects of business.

Scott Simms, senior public information officer for Portland General Electric, points out that "research drives what we do." He adds:

> We track corporate favorability and general impressions of the company. We conduct focus groups about new product and service offerings as well as company and industry issues. We do satisfaction surveys among opinion leaders in government, business, community, the energy sector, etc. Virtually everything we do here is driven by research. Otherwise, why waste your time and other people's time trying to guess what your customers are thinking, your employees are feeling, and the public is reacting to?

Virginia McCarty, who is CEO, McCarty and Associates, Inc., a marketing firm in Seattle, Wash., also says it is crucial to learn about research.

Students who plan to become communication professionals truly need to understand the importance of research and application of that research. In communications, research should be the basis in all approaches. Consumer options and patterns are where every project should begin. It is paramount to know what motivates our audiences to respond, listen or apply.

Janay Collins, senior product manager at Microsoft Corporation, elaborates on the relation between research and business objectives.

Managers and other professionals need to focus on defining why they need the research in the first place — what action they will take from the results and how is it prioritized against the overall goals of the business. A well-managed research plan should coherently deliver on the business objectives. Finally, having defined the research goals and prioritized them within the business, the clients need to recognize the time (in weeks, not days) that it takes to put together a proper research project, and extract actionable steps from the results.

The late David Ogilvy, one of the founders of the advertising agency that bears his name (Ogilvy and Mather) and one of *AdWeek*'s most influential advertisers, was a strong advocate of using research to support creative decisions.

Advertising people who ignore research are as dangerous as generals who ignore decodes of enemy signals.

In sum, these professionals say that research drives much of what they do, that managers and other professions also need to be able to define their needs and goals in relation to research, and that it's dangerous to ignore research. Guessing is not sufficient. Good research is necessary to understand the marketplace. You'll need to understand what constitutes appropriate research and the type of methodology (e.g., survey, a focus group, or Internet study) you'll need to solve problems. As Collins stresses, you'll have to prioritize your research objectives and clearly define your research needs and goals, which is the first step in the research process described in Chapter 3.

RESEARCH REDUCES BIAS

Bias is anything that interferes with making a rational decision. We are all biased in some ways. For example, some students think professors are forgetful. Some professors think students just want to party. These biases can interfere with successfully predicting how people will behave or the consequences of ad campaigns and other communication actions. We should strive to reduce bias as much as possible.

Bias makes it difficult to get an objective analysis. For example, after seeing our latest creative effort, will our friends tell us we did a mediocre job? Not likely. Even if we seek other opinions by stopping shoppers in a local mall, can we conclude that these opinions accurately reflect the entire marketplace? Again, the answer is "no."

I worked on an audience study about a decade ago where many people said they thought their local newscast was "sensational." If you assume "sensational" news is bad, then you'd recommend that the TV station change its content to reduce sensationalism. But that change is based on the biased interpretation that "sensational" news is bad. What if the audience thinks it is good? In fact, follow-up research found that about half of the audience liked "sensational" news. So reducing "sensational" news might lead to a smaller audience, which would be a bad decision if the goal is to maintain or increase audience size.

Personal biases are those we carry inside of us, our beliefs about how the world works. They can make it difficult for us to understand different cultures. For example, research shows that people tend to associate with other people who have similar politics, ethics, habits and activities. This limits our contact and interaction with people who have different opinions, values, behaviors and tastes. Our biases can lead us to seek only the information that confirms our view of the world (called "confirmation bias"). Consider the issue of student drinking. Despite the reality that most college students do not drink to excess, if we only pay attention to news reports and media images, we could easily come to the opposite conclusion — that irresponsible drinking is the norm.

Some biases don't matter much. For example, you might believe that German chocolate cake comes from Germany, when the truth is that it actually got its name from an American whose last name was "German." But biases can become serious when they affect your life. For instance, if you think there is a lot of crime in your neighborhood, even if there isn't, you might restrict your travel or experience undue stress.

External bias is information we get from outside ourselves. It affects how we view the world, and it can fool us into making bad decisions. There can be bias in how we obtain information and how we conduct research. External bias can come in the form of misinformation. Perhaps we used census data to describe the Las Vegas market, but if the data were five years old, then it was fairly useless for such a fast-growing market. Maybe we did focus groups with 44 shoppers at the Mall of America, but do those 44 really represent all people in the market?

These examples illustrate that we need to be careful in applying our

JOEY REAGAN

assumptions and beliefs. To the communication professional, bias can interfere with how we evaluate ourselves, our work, target audiences and campaigns. Research, correctly conducted and applied, can help reduce biases. We can help that process by:

- Being analytical and skeptical,
- Being skeptical of our own view of the world,
- Being open to alternative perspectives,
- Being skeptical of others' views, including experts,
- Being careful in the application of information, including research.

By subjecting our beliefs, the information we acquire, and even our own work to verification, we can make better decisions. A major component of the verification strategy is to seek other viewpoints, modify our conclusions, and then subject those conclusions to scientific scrutiny. In communication studies, we subject our conclusions to *social science*, which is the study of and prediction of people's behavior.

TRADITIONAL WAYS OF KNOWING

People try to determine how the world works in an number of ways. These ways include tenacity, authority, intuition and science.

Tenacity is based on believing something just because the belief has been around a long time or has been often repeated. It is difficult to counter because of a psychological condition called "belief-perseverance" — a tendency to believe despite contrary evidence. Examples include:

- Students can leave a classroom if the teacher is late, but they have to wait longer if they are full professors.
- As long as one doesn't charge money, it's OK to use copyrighted material.
- There are more crimes during a full moon.

Authority is based on trusting the source. Trusted sources include ministers, judges, experts and even professors. Trusting the source can lead to accepting misinformation. For example, an expert might tell you that humorous ads attract more attention than serious ads, but without verifying this, would you create a humorous ad for a funeral home?

Intuition is an internal belief, a gut feeling or personal insight. This includes "common sense." Intuition is difficult to counter because of "confirmation bias" —

a tendency to only look for evidence that supports our intuition and other defenses we erect to protect our beliefs.

This may not be a problem if the outcome is minimal. Betting and losing $5 on the Giants isn't a big deal to most people. But would you "bet" $85,000 on an advertising campaign just because your intuition tells you it will work. Do you really want city hall to spend millions of dollars on a new civic center because they "think" it will attract conventions? Should your company invest in an expensive high-speed network just because your gut feelings tell you it will make employees more productive?

The problem with the above three methods of knowing is that they are difficult to "falsify." That is, they do not have a method for determining the truth or falsehood of a proposition or belief. For example, you can't falsify the belief that there are more crimes during a full moon unless you check data on crime compared to phases of the moon. When you do that (i.e., engage in empirical observation), you are no longer relying on tenacity but are employing scientific methods of research.

COMMON SENSE MAY BE WRONG

We are all tempted to think that our understanding of the world is accurate. We often say, "It wouldn't have happened if they had just used common sense."

Yet much of what we think makes sense is simply wrong. For instance, many people in the United States think that water going down a drain spins in a counterclockwise direction because of the spin of the earth. The "Coriolis effect" is extended to water in a basin. While the Coriolis effect impacts large systems like the Earth's atmosphere, it has little effect on drains because other factors, like the shape of the basin, have a greater impact.

Beliefs in myths like this have a minor impact on most people's lives. But other beliefs can have major impacts on public policy or our lives. For example, many people believe that humans only use 10 percent of their brains. But brain imaging (MRI and PET scans) and electrical stimulation of the brain show that the vast majority of the brain is used. If legislators believed the myth, they presumably would be more likely to spend sizable public funds on commercial techniques to increase brain usage among school children. And if you believed the myth, you might waste a lot of money for online drugs, juices and other so-called brain boosters.

Science Is ...

The alternative to foundering with our beliefs is to use science. For purposes here, science will be defined as observation, identification, description, investigation, and explanation of phenomena. To do science, a study must have the following characteristics:

- Empiricism
- Objectivity
- Testability
- Falsifiability

Empiricism means "observing." Instead of only thinking about an issue or asking others what they think, you observe the phenomenon. Observing includes "to look at" as a way to empirically assess people's behavior, but the term includes many other methods of observation. We can ask people questions to "observe" their attitudes. We can have people fill out a test to "observe" their knowledge.

Objectivity does not mean that researchers have no biases. Rather, it means that we employ methods to reduce our biases and make those methods public so that others can evaluate and replicate the research.

Testability means that you observe phenomena that are amenable to measurement. For example, most external human behavior is measurable (e.g., purchase behavior) while some internal thought processes are not (e.g., communicating with the dead).

Falsifiability means that your conclusions can be disproved. It is intrinsically linked to the three elements listed above. Science means making those methods available to other researchers so others can criticize as well as replicate your study to see if the same results can be achieved.

The ultimate goals of science are explanation and prediction. Your research ideally should help explain people's attitudes and behavior while also predicting future behavior. This helps test whether your conclusions are correct (falsifiable).

You'll Have to Work with Research

Regardless of how you feel now about research, you will have to deal with it in the real world. You probably will have to work with a research director, read and apply research reports, and evaluate your work with research. You may have to work with a research team when your clients demand facts and figures. You may be asked to provide input for your company's research projects.

You will have to understand your client's needs and goals. You will have to communicate those needs and goals to the research people, prioritize those needs (because you can't do everything in one project), understand what constitutes good research, know whether the project will be practical in terms of time and money, and know whether you have met the goals.

ELECTRONICS ARE CHANGING YOUR WORLD

Within the last decade, major changes have taken place in the field of research. This includes the trend toward online focus groups, electronic data collection, doing analyses in your own spreadsheet, and the impact of new technologies, like cell phones, on telephone research.

You need to keep up with the changes and respond to them. Research will help. Not only will you need to follow media coverage of your company or changes in your market, you may have to deal with problems caused by the Internet. One new type of problem you will probably encounter is negative electronic publicity. For example, Target Corporation found itself faced with e-mail claims that it did not contribute to veterans' causes, and Starbucks faced assertions that it refused to send free coffee to U.S. soldiers serving in Iraq.

Dealing with these potential problems will require more than a gut feeling. You'll need to know what was written, how extensively it has been distributed, whether it has had an impact and, if so, if there anything you can do about it?

CHAPTER 2

A BRIEF HISTORY OF COMMUNICATION RESEARCH

O ne chapter cannot adequately cover the history of the development of communication research. However, it is important to know something of its history if only to appreciate the idea that communication research has a tradition — an accumulated body of knowledge (which is a hallmark of science) — and to understand why it has various methods and uses.

Communication research owes its development to other disciplines, primarily other social and physical sciences. Of course, once established, communication research developed its own lines of inquiry just like other disciplines. The histories of other disciplines, such as marketing research, overlap with communication research but are not covered here.

Communication research has two main emphases or applications: *academic communication research* and *applied communication research*. The former is closer to the social sciences of sociology, political science and psychology, as well as to some qualitative approaches like ethnic studies. The latter is closer to marketing research in business and finance. But both areas overlap. For example, recent theories that explain the impact of technologies on society grew out of audience studies for cable television and other media, and advertising studies about the impact of campaigns borrowed heavily from academic work in psychology and advertising research in business schools.

The following summaries are based on various sources that you are encouraged to consult along with many others that you can find on the Internet. These sources include "Timeline for the history of science and social science" (http://www.mdx.ac.uk/www/study/sshtim.htm), "The History of Science" from *Wikipedia* (http://www.wikipedia.com), Houghton-Mifflin's online "Readers Companion to American History," Everett M. Rogers' *A History of Communication Study* (New York: Free Press, 1997), and an online summary by Em Griffin, "A First Look at Communication Theory" (www.afirstlook.com/archive /talkabout.cfm?source=archther).

HISTORY OF SCIENCE

For thousands of years humans have inquired into the nature of the universe. Originally, the inquiry was philosophical, characterized by tenacity, authority, and intuition, and some observation without the modern methods of science. In other words, *reasoning* was the primary method used to explain how the universe worked, including inductive and deductive reasoning. Reasoning is an important element of science, but the early philosophers didn't often engage in empirical observation and, as a consequence, often reached incorrect conclusions, such as the idea that "heavier bodies fall faster than lighter bodies."

The scientific revolution in the 16th and 17th centuries, led by European scientists like Copernicus, Newton, Galileo and Kepler, moved science from philosophy to a mathematical, mechanical and empirical field of study. This is not to say that there were no studies before this period or in other parts of the world that tried to break away from the philosophical tradition. The concept of "zero," for example, was first recorded in Mesopotamia around 3 B.C. and in India in the mid-fifth century. It spread to Cambodia in the 7th century and into China and the Middle East by the 8th century, but didn't reach western Europe until the 12th century. "Algorithm," named for a Persian mathematician, consists of logic and repeatable steps that lead to a specific outcome. The Middle East also developed the use of citations and peer review.

The 19th and 20th centuries saw the expansion of the explanatory power of chemistry and physics through an understanding of electricity and the atom, the unification of mass and energy, and great strides also were made in geology, medicine, and other areas.

HISTORY OF SOCIAL SCIENCE

Social science as the study of human groups arose in the West during the nineteenth century as an attempt to apply the progress made in the natural sciences to humans. European social scientists had a more philosophical orientation while American social scientists focused more on data-gathering. This essentially marks the distinction between the major methods of social science: qualitative (philosophically and critically oriented and focused on interpreting words and actions) and quantitative (numerically oriented). Both are used by scholars the world over.

In the United States between 1880 and World War I, a variety of professional organizations and social science journals were founded (e.g., American Political Science Association, American Sociological Society, *American Journal of Sociology* and *American Political Science Review*). Also academic departments were established in universities (e.g., economics, sociology, and psychology). The hope of social scientists at the time was that research would solve social problems like poverty and crime.

In the early 1900s, social science research was exemplified by quantitative studies like those of voting behavior. The role of qualitative research is illustrated by the work by anthropologist Margaret Mead, combining reports of fieldwork in the South Pacific with social criticism concerning basic values. This sparked controversy in the social sciences. Moralists were accused of not being scientific enough. Conversely, "pure" social scientists were accused of being narrow and unjustly claiming to use the methods of the natural sciences.

HISTORY OF COMMUNICATION RESEARCH

Communication research has its roots in ancient Greece, where the study of rhetoric, which is the art of effective speaking and persuasion, was a central subject for most students. That was the essence of communication research until about a century ago, when speech communication began to emerge as a distinct academic field.

For the first half of the last century, college speech teachers were usually members of English departments. Speech teachers stressed oral performance and began communication's first professional group, the National Association of Academic Teachers of Public Speaking, which published the *Quarterly Journal of Public Speaking*. The focus was on giving practical advice to those trying to influence audiences through public address, radio announcing, drama, and other applications. The intellectual foundation for the discipline primarily came from the writings of Plato, Aristotle, Cicero, and other historical rhetors.

Communication studies as a social science began to emerge after 1930. Wilbur

Schramm, director of the Stanford Institute for Communication Research, identifies four men from that era as the "founding fathers" of communication research: (1) political scientist Harold Lasswell, who analyzed Nazi propaganda; (2) social psychologist Kurt Lewin, who investigated prejudice and the way groups influence the decisions of individual members; (3) sociologist Paul Lazarsfeld, founder of the the Bureau of Applied Social Research at Columbia University, who tested theories about marketing along with pioneering innovative survey and focus-group techniques to evaluate the emotional impact of broadcasting; and (4) experimental psychologist Carl Hovland, who tested the persuasive effects of source credibility (the believability of a speaker) and the order of arguments within a message.

During this time, other fields of study also influenced communication studies. In the 1940s, Claude Shannon and Warren Weaver drew on mathematics to develop an information model that attempted to measure noise in electrical transmissions for the purpose of improving Bell System's telephone service. It focused on two parts: how much information can be communicated within a system and what parts of the system affect the communication flow. Although Shannon said that human communication was outside the scope of his model, many communication scholars have studied his model and adapted it to communication research. For example, David Berlo used it in 1960 for the famous "SMCR model of communication" (source-message-channel-receiver), and Harold Laswell extended it to his famous definition of communication: "Who says what to whom via what channels with what effect?"

Communication studies as a formal discipline within the university began to emerge after Wilbur Schramm and other social scientists met to discuss issues during World War II. At that time, there were no doctoral programs in communication, and many undergraduate programs resided in journalism programs. By the late 1940s, some Big 10 schools like University of Iowa and University of Wisconsin had created Ph.D. programs in mass communication.

The period 1950 to 1970 also saw a great deal of growth in the discipline. Many colleges and universities offered courses in "Public Address," "Oral Interpretation," "Argumentation and Debate," "Persuasion," "History of American Public Address," and "Classical Rhetoric." But during the 1960s big changes took place. Many schools replaced "Public Speaking" with "Interpersonal Communication." Interpersonal and media communication were hot topics. Oral interpretation and public address were not. Voice and drama courses were housed in speech departments or in completely separate departments. Communication programs were established at Iowa and Illinois, and the first department of communication and college of communication were created at Michigan State University.

Communication research also owes a lot to sociology. In the 1920s, several sociologists at the universities of Michigan and Chicago began examining the impact of mass media. Psychology contributed as well by doing experiments that assessed the meaning of communication. By mid-century these fundamental studies had evolved into more obvious communication areas like "propaganda," and, by the 1970s, "agenda setting" was a big topic of study.

The development of communication research programs was not without some problems. Tension often existed between professionals and scientists and between qualitative vs. quantitative approaches. To some extent the dichotomies are real, but many programs and researchers have been able to straddle the boundaries. After all, quantitative scholars have used qualitative studies to develop their questionnaires and scales, and qualitative scholars often point to surveys and experiments to support their arguments.

Once communication became established as an academic discipline in universities, it was free to pursue its own lines of inquiry, although it did not abandon traditional lines like "agenda setting." New inquiries examined such topics as "information source selection" in the 1960s and 1970s, and "cable TV, Internet and other technology adoption" in the 1980s, 1990s and 2000s. Of course, now there are hundreds of lines of study.

THE FUTURE OF COMMUNICATION RESEARCH

There will continue to be the discussion of where communication study belongs. Is it a humanity or a social science? Should theoretical studies be in communication departments and professional studies in business and journalism schools? Or should they all be together?

There is no crystal ball but trends can be identified. Two major traditions in communication research have emerged in the last 50 years. The first derives its background from rhetorical studies, and it now is manifest primarily in "communication studies." The second has a more professional tradition, arising out of studies in marketing, industry research, and advertising and public relations in communication departments.

There will remain, on one hand, some tension between the academic community and private industry. Some academicians want to keep their disciplines "pure," eschewing the "bottom line" mentality of industry, while some professionals lament academics' lack of understanding of media industries about which academicians conduct their research. Yet, on the other hand, there is a lot of cooperation between professionals and academics. This includes professional associations that offer research grants to universities, such as the National Association of Broadcasters' "Grants for Research in Broadcasting," and professors who consult with industry to make applied research more valid.

CHAPTER 3

THE RESEARCH PROCESS

Ａs noted in Chapter 1, you, the communication professional, will have to help develop the research plan and goals and will have to understand the research process so that appropriate methods can be selected. In addition, you need to know whether the project is doable; that is, can the budget support it and is there enough time to do the research properly?

The following guide will help you make sure your projects are achievable, and the guide can be used as a sort-of table of contents to this book.

STEPS IN THE RESEARCH PROCESS

Figure 3.1 on the next page shows step-by-step the process of research. Starting at the wrong step or skipping a step can lead waste time or money. For example, if you skip the first five steps, jumping immediately to Step 6 and decide to do a telephone poll, you might spends thousands of dollars on a research project and get valid results but then have no place to apply those results because you had no goal (see Step 1).

Having said that, I need to make two important points. First, you can't help but mull over the steps out of order. For example, you will be thinking about variables even as you write your needs and goals or develop your research questions, but you'll finalize them later when you *operationalize*. And second, you need to know all of the steps before you can realistically do step one; that is, you

Define this Term!!!

Figure 3.1
STEPS IN THE RESEARCH PROCESS

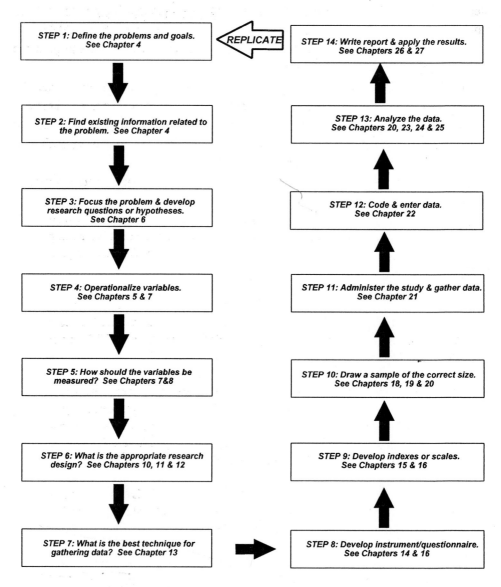

cannot know if your project is doable if you don't have a sense of what designs and techniques are available and what resources are required for them. There is also some overlap; Chapter 20 ("Sampling Error and Sample Size") relates to an early step, "Draw a sample of correct size," and a later step, "Analyze the Data.." But don't jump around the steps arbitrarily because that can adversely affect the validity of your project.

In this book chapters also are devoted to issues that do not fit easily into the steps in Figure 3.1 because they are designed for understanding concepts (e.g., cause-and-effect [Chapter 9], how normal probability applies to sampling [Chapter 17)], application examples [Chapter 27], ethics [Chapter 28] and where to get more information about research [Chapter 29]).

I would like to preface each step above by saying, "This step is crucial." Ignoring one can ruin your entire project. You may choose to skip a step only if you cannot use it. For example, you may choose not to use a scale (Step 9), but you must consider first whether the complexity of your variables warrants using scales. In many cases there are implications for other steps.

With these caveats in mind, let's look at each of the steps in more depth.

STEP 1: Define the problems and goals. You will identify why you need to do research and how you will use the results. If you have no clear goals for using the results, you should not be doing research in the first place. Write down your needs and goals.

STEP 2: Find existing information. You might find some possible solutions to your problems by examining previous research. In addition, you need to know what other researchers have done so you don't "reinvent the wheel." This can save you time and money.

STEP 3: Focus the problem and develop research questions or hypotheses. You need to be specific in order to identify which variables, measures, designs, etc., are related to your needs and goals. This is usually done with "research questions," if you are charting new ground, and with "hypotheses," if you have found a body of consistent research in Step 2.

STEP 4: Operationalize variables. Define each variable. This is not always as easy as it seems. "Income" may be simple, but "factors," "image," "attention to my ad" and others can be difficult to define.

STEP 5: How should the variables be measured? Merely identifying variables is not sufficient. Do you eventually need averages or percentages, or just the words people say? Should you have categories or real numbers? Do you need to do a scale or will one question be sufficient?

STEP 6: What is the appropriate research design? Should it be a focus group, a survey, an experiment, or a case study? Qualitative or quantitative? There are many designs from which to choose.

STEP 7: What is the best technique for gathering data? Should it be in-person, or telephone, mail, or electronic (e.g., Internet)? Each has advantages and disadvantages.

STEP 8: Develop the instrument or questionnaire. Will you be using a mail questionnaire, a Web-based questionnaire, a focus group agenda, or what?

STEP 9: Develop indexes or scales. Not all variables can be measured with just one question. Attitudes, opinions, knowledge, lifestyle and other variables can be very complex, requiring multiple questions (or measures). If you need more than one question to define a single variable, you should consider creating scales.

STEP 10: Draw a sample of the correct size. Should you use a sample? If so, what kind and what size? How do you know it represents the population?

STEP 11: Administer the study and gather data. Merely collecting data is not enough. How do you know it's being collected correctly? Is the study proceeding according to schedule? How can you be sure your consultant is doing his or her job?

STEP 12: Code and enter data. While you hope your consultant or research department is doing this for you, do you understand what the numbers (codes) mean? Will you be able to get the analysis you need? If you have words as data do you need to make categories for them?

STEP 13: Analyze the data. Here you find out the answers to your research questions or hypotheses. Here you also have to temper your interpretation of the results when you decide if relations between variables exist and whether they are important. Your knowledge of concepts like "cause-and-effect," "generalizability," "significance" and "explained variance" is crucial here.

STEP 14: Write report and apply the results. A report is more than just a cluster of tables. It should also contain information about why and how the study was done. You should retain all data, questionnaires and other project material. Of course, the report is of no use unless it is applied to solve the problems and achieve the goals you identified in Step 1.

REPLICATE. The last step points back to Step 1. Remember from Chapter 2 that science is testable and falsifiable. This is where that takes place. You

Table 3.1
EXAMPLE OF SURVEY BUDGET

Office phone/LD	$25.00
Office supplies	20.00
Mail	40.00
Travel	65.00
Hotel	200.00
Meals	60.00
Purchase RDD sample	800.00
Sub-contract data collection (phone center/CATI)	4,000.00
TOTAL	$5,210.00
Consulting (design, questionnaire, analysis, report)	$9,000.00
GRAND TOTAL	$14,210.00

replicate because research is never 100 percent correct; it is subject to many types of errors (sampling error, limits on the frame, and so on, covered in later chapters) and we are only "probably sure" of the results. So you need to regularly conduct research to verify your results or look for changes.

A major consideration of any project is budget, both time and money. At any step you should be thinking about this so you don't waste effort on research fantasies. Some projects can take more than a month (see the timeline in Chapter 21), and research often is expensive as illustrated by the budget in Table 3.1 for a simple one-shot survey of 300 respondents.

Chapter 4

Defining the Problem and Finding Existing Information

Validate the Assumption here.

*D*on't get ahead of yourself is good advice to follow when conducting research. I once talked with a potential client who asked me about doing a telephone survey of radio listeners to find out if a new competitor was eating into his station's audience. When we backed up to Step 1, we learned that a weak transmitter was creating much of the problem, and moving the transmitter tower or increasing its power was the first consideration, not research. This illustrates again why it is so important to first define your problems and goals.

Defining the problem should identify the information needed and the goals for using that information. Without a problem definition, your research will be unguided, and the results may not be applicable to your needs. Without goals, you can spend a lot of time and money for data that apply to nothing. Write down the ideas into a *problem statement*. Exchange it with your staff, colleagues, consultant or research director. Come back to your problem statement and revise it.

Generating Problems and Goals

Some problems are easy to identify, like a sudden drop in revenue or a startling increase in negative stories in the media. These are only potential problems, because until you gather more information you don't know the extent of the problem, what might be causing it, or indeed if there is a problem in the first place. Is the drop in revenue just a cyclical variation in sales? Did any customers even read the negative stories?

Potential problems can be identified by a virtually unlimited number of sources. These sources include:

- Your advertisers
- Customer comments
- Your own observations
- Your staff
- External analysts and experts
- Brainstorming
- Your annual report
- Other research you've conducted
- Trade publication stories
- Your family and friends
- Your local newscast
- Articles you've read in the newspaper

PROBLEM STATEMENT EXAMPLES

Problem statements are specific written expressions that contain two elements: (1) a clear exposition of the need, and (2) a clear articulation of the goals for the use of information you gather about the problem.

Problems can be simple such as, "I'm new to the market and need to know its demographic makeup," or more complex: "Opinions about my company have changed. Why?" Gathering information about these problems should help you make better decisions about your market or campaigns. In many cases you may identify multiple problems. So multiple problem statements may be combined into a single research project, or you may find several projects are necessary to examine all of the problems. Below are three examples of problem statements. In each case the overall projects involved more than one statement. These have been simplified for the examples.

WHY AM I DOING this?
WHAT ARE my GOALS?

EXAMPLE A

A local weekly newspaper found that local advertisers were becoming as sophisticated as larger national and multinational organizations in their demand for information about their readers. At a weekly meeting, the paper's sales staff revealed that local advertisers were reluctant to purchase ad space because the sales people could not provide information about the readership, including demographics and purchase behavior. Although the paper's managers believed their readers were an upscale, highly educated part of the community, there was no hard evidence to support that. Based on the advertisers' and sales staff's comments, the publisher defined a straightforward problem.

> *Problem Statement:* We need to know the demographics (education, income, etc.) of our readers and their expected purchase behavior (auto, clothing, etc.), along with readership (weeks per month read, sections read, pass along, etc.) in order to assist the sales staff in targeting dealerships, retail clothing outlets and other local advertisers.

Notice that the problem statement includes a section about the needed information (demographics, purchase behavior and readership) and a section about the goal for using that information (to assist the sales staff in targeting local advertisers). The statement suggests that a simple readership study — one that would survey readers about their income, age and other demographics and their expected purchases of autos, clothing, etc. — would work best.

EXAMPLE B

Some problems are more complex and go beyond simple descriptions of a population. A regional hospital's public relations director noted that revenue at the hospital had flattened and attributed that drop to increased competition in the local market. Other hospitals in the region were advertising more aggressively. In addition, national surveys reported in trade publications indicated that patient images of hospitals in general were shaped by interactions with the staff, the so-called "bedside manner."

> *Problem Statement:* Kadlec Medical Center, a regional hospital in Tri-Cities, Washington, needs to know what factors are important when patients select a hospital. Do those factors conform to results from national surveys? Kadlec needs this information in order to know what to emphasize in its advertising and promotional campaigns in order increase bed use.

This example contains a "relational" issue rather than merely a descriptive one. It implies more difficult research than Example A because you would have to, first, identify the factors people use to select a hospital; second, develop ways to measure the importance of those factors; and, third, relate those factors to hospital selection.

EXAMPLE C

The King County Council of Camp Fire (now the Central Puget Sound Council) is a nonprofit youth organization. To raise money, the organization creates campaigns aimed at government and private funding agencies (many of which require demonstration of service to both boys and girls), volunteers, members and potential members. The organization noted that some of its programs had low participation, and it suspected that the traditional name associated with the organization, Camp Fire *Girls,* might explain the low participation of boys. The organization had no other research to draw upon that examined these issues.

> *Problem Statement:* Camp Fire needs to know some basic information along with variables that affect participation and donation. The focus is on the general public (both parents and children) in the counties it serves, its members (both parents and child members) and potential corporate contributors or volunteers. Are they aware of Camp Fire? What does Camp Fire mean to them? Are they aware of the various programs that Camp Fire has for adults and children, boys and girls, different ages groups, and different needs? Answers to these questions will identify targets and will help guide the emphasis of the promotional campaigns targeted to each group.

This project required a more complex research project because it involved multiple target groups, relations (factors affecting participation and donation by multiple targets), and more variables (awareness of brand, awareness of programs, etc.).

FIND EXISTING INFORMATION

It is important to search for available information about your needs and goals (Step 2). Perhaps national studies have been conducted on some of the issues identified in your problem statement. Maybe you have research that your company conducted several years ago. Look through syndicated research. While ratings and other narrowly descriptive numbers may not solve your problem, they can give good descriptions of your market. Archives like the Census Bureau and city and county clerks' offices can provide good descriptions of your overall market. And don't forget the scientific literature in journals and books.

Even if you can't find existing relevant research directly related to your needs, previous research can show you how to ask questions, provide existing scales to measure image, and so on, so you don't have to waste time developing those.

STOP AND THINK

At this point, it is wise to think about the costs of your study and its feasibility. Think about possible variables and research questions. Are they measurable and answerable? Is it realistic to proceed?

A *research plan* can help answer those questions, and it is essential to any project you undertake. Such a plan tentatively lays out the expected research questions, research design, data collection technique, analysis, etc., along with expected costs and time involved. Remember, you should stop any time in the research process when the study outstrips your resources or when you realize that continuing would be futile.

CHAPTER 5

AN INTRODUCTION TO VARIABLES AND VARIANCE

I introduce variables here, before Step 3, because you must always be thinking, "What are the variables?" If you cannot identify variables in your problem statement, you should not do research. After all, the focus of all research is on variables and variance.

A *variable* is anything that varies; *variance* is how much something varies. Think about it. You want to know how people change, not how they stay the same. If people's buying habits were constant, you would know exactly what they plan to purchase. You would not care about campaigns because there is no change. But people do change. They change when their lives change, when they get new information, when they are emotionally evolved, when their friends influence them, and when they grow older.

If people didn't change, there would be "zero variance." The importance of knowing how much people change is to know what the impact of that change is or what the impact of your campaign is. You'd like to know whether to expect sales to increase 1 percent or 20 percent, whether you need a 5 percent change in voters or a 25 percent change to win the election, or whether your promotional campaign improved the image of your company 1 percent or 15 percent.

It is by knowing variables and how much they vary that you determine what causes people to change, how much they change and whether or not what you did caused that change to happen.

THE IMPORTANCE OF VARIABLES

Variables are intimately involved with all stages of the research process. You need to think "variables" when you write down your needs, when you create questionnaires, when you do analysis, and every other step. You'll need to fully understand your variables or you won't be able to write good questions for your questionnaire (e.g., do you need categories of income or exact dollar amounts?) and you won't be able to determine whether to do an experiment or survey (e.g., you can't randomly assign gender but you can randomly assign viewership of your ad for an experiment).

After you have clearly defined your needs and goals and focused on research questions or hypotheses, you have to precisely define variables so that everyone involved in the project or reading the report will know what the data mean. You should know, for example, if "income" means household or personal income, and if it's measured in categories and the values of those categories. Before you can write research questions or hypotheses about relations between variables, you need to know what variables are implied by your needs and goals.

CONCEPTUALIZING VARIABLES

Conceptualizing a variable is not always as easy as it seems. For example, try to identify the variables in the following:

> Among women, 18-34 years old, 68 percent are aware of my company's participation in the community fund-raiser.

I deliberately threw in the plural "variables" as a trick. There is only *one* variable, "awareness of participation in the fund-raiser," because it is the only term allowed to vary (people can be aware or not aware). "Among women" and "18-34" merely define the target population. Men and other age categories are excluded. Terms that are not allowed to vary are called *constants*. The obvious reason that these are not variables is that they have only one category, and, thus, they do not meet the definition of a variable. Examples of variables and constants are found in Table 5.1.

OPERATIONALIZING VARIABLES

Operationalization means to create a definition for a variable that can be used in research and relates to the needs and goals of your study. In other words, to put the

Table 5.1

LISTS OF VARIABLES AND CONSTANTS

Variables	Constants/Targets
Gender	Men
Age	Over 50
Television viewing	View TV more than 3 hours/day
Image of my company	Has a positive image of my company
Reasons for not exercising	Exercisers
Children vs. adults	18-35 year olds

variable into operation. Details about operationalizing are in Chapter 7.

There is no best operationalization. It depends upon how you conceptualize or define your variables. As long as the measures you create are useful for testing your research questions or hypotheses, then they are good. Also remember that there are multiple definitions for any variables (e.g., "age" can be in categories or real years). If you can't create an operational definition for a variable that someone else can understand, then you have failed.

VARIANCE

Variance is the amount of variability in your variable. On one hand, suppose you were assessing how many hours people spend using the Internet each day. If most people spend two hours, only a few spend zero, one or three hours, and no one spends more than three hours, there would be little variability. Consequently, you would have a small range in which to differentiate people. On the other hand, if you were measuring age of adults in the general population, you would have many people at many ages from 18 to 100+. You would have a large variability — a very wide range to work with.

Statistically, variance means the dispersion around the average (statisticians call the average the "mean"). The larger the variance, the more widely scattered the values around the mean.

The concept of variance is important later in Chapter 24 when you read about *explained variance*. As a researcher you want to explain why variability occurs, so you need to discover how much variability there is and how much of that variability you can explain or predict.

Let's take a practical example. Suppose you want to know about people's perceptions of your company. You would probably create a scale to measure the image of your company — perhaps it would have a range of values from 1 to 10, with one meaning "poor" and 10 meaning "very good." That doesn't mean people will extend over all those values. It's possible that people have a very positive image of your company and the real range in the population might be from 8 to 10. That's a small range, and you would just note that this seems positive and stop at that.

But if you found there was a large variability — some very negative, some very positive, and some in between — you would have a range of numbers more like 2 to 10. Then you would want to know what's causing the variability. Are males more negative than females? Do those who saw your campaign rate your company more positively than those who didn't? Is it the weather? Is it how much news coverage you got?

Merely identifying those causes is not enough. You need to know which of them are more important and how important they are. That's where explained variance comes in, because it tells you how much of the variability in image is explained by each variable or by all the variables taken together. Even if you found out that your campaign had an impact on image, if that impact was only 1 percent, then you might not be very confident in the success of your campaign compared to the impact being 15 percent.

There is a phenomenon in statistics that if the sample is large enough, all variables are "statistically significantly related" to each other. Unfortunately, most of those relations are trivial. That is, they share little variance with each other. Looking at variance will help you detect which three or four or five relations are the strongest and, therefore, the most important for you to use to make decisions.

CHAPTER 6

RESEARCH QUESTIONS AND HYPOTHESES

Having thought about the variables implied in your needs statement, you are ready to make the transition between understanding your needs and goals and the development of your *research questions* (RQs) and/or *hypotheses* (Hs). RQs and Hs help narrow and focus your needs. Once you have written RQs or Hs, you will need to define or "operationalize" your variables (see Chapter 7).

DESCRIPTIVE VS. RELATIONAL RESEARCH

Before writing RQs or Hs, you need to make sure you understand what kind of questions you are contemplating: descriptive or relational or both.

Descriptive research — and descriptive RQs — are just that: describing a population. Although you may ask many questions and have many separate variables, you are only interested in one variable at a time. For example, you may want to know the demographics of your market. You only describe average income, percent male, percent owning a home, average number of children and so on.

Relational research — and its Hs and its relational RQs — look at how variables change together, in relation to each other. So that means examining two or more variables at the same time. For example, if you wanted to know how demographics related to each other in your market, you should compare gender and income (do males have higher income than do females?), marital status and home ownership (does a higher percentage of married people own homes than unmarried people?), and so on.

WHAT IS A HYPOTHESIS?

Research questions can be either descriptive or relational, but hypotheses are always relational. A *hypothesis* is a causal statement about a relation between two variables. At least one of the variables is an *independent* variable (IV) and at least one is a *dependent* variable (DV). An *independent variable* is the presumed cause, and the *dependent variable* is the presumed effect.

For example, you might expect that people with higher incomes are more likely to buy a Porsche than people with lower incomes. You expect income to affect the decision to purchase a Porsche. So income is the IV and buying a Porsche is the DV.

A hypothesis is the most formal statement that a researcher can make about relations among variables. Hypotheses are used to predict results in a research project. They ideally are made before data collection and should be based on the problem statement. And they are often derived from previous research; that is, a hypothesis is derived from a theory or it is generalized from a body of previous research. Thus, a hypothesis is:

- a statement
- based on previous research or a theory
- about a causal relation
- between two or more variables, one of which is the independent variable (IV) and the other of which is the dependent variable (DV)
- amenable to research and replication.

The best way to test a hypothesis is with an experiment. However, many hypotheses cannot be tested with experiments because you cannot control the IV. That is, you cannot randomly assign various levels or categories of the IV to subjects. For example, if you expect the image of your company to affect how often people shop at your store, you cannot randomly assign the image people hold inside their brains.

The following example of a hypothesis is derived from "Diffusion Theory" which is characterized by various chronological stages of adoption, including "innovators, early adopters, early majority, late majority, and laggards." If you are promoting a new invention you could use the theory to predict that the first buyers would be "innovators" and "early adopters." The theory and its related body of research characterize early adopters as venturesome, who are able to understand and apply complex technical knowledge, are able to cope with a high degree of uncertainty about an innovation, and have success in careers and income. Thinking about variables ("operationalizations" will take place later), you can already identify several: adoption (whether or not), venturesomeness, amount of technical knowledge, amount of uncertainty tolerated, employment status, and income. Likewise, several hypotheses can be derived. Try to identify the DV and IV in each.

H1:   Those likely to adopt my invention are more venturesome compared to those not likely to adopt.

H2:   Those likely to adopt my invention have higher incomes compared to those not likely to adopt.

In both of the hypotheses the DV is "likelihood of adoption." In H1, the IV is "venturesomeness," and in H2, the IV is "income."

An example of a hypothesis generalized from a body of research comes from research on information source use. Since the 1950s, it has been clear that the most frequently cited sources for information about what's going on in the world today are newspapers and television (see, e.g., Roper polls and other studies), but other research shows that different sources are used when specific information is sought. For example, when seeking financial information people are more likely to use media like phone and Internet over newspapers and TV. But there is no "theory of information source use." In general, the body of research shows that "mass" media are more used for general topics and "narrow" media are used for specific topics. The expectation may be that the topic causes people to select different media. Thus, a hypothesis may be derived that says:

H3:   People are more likely to select the Internet, magazines and human sources over TV, newspapers and radio as sources for information about personal financial investments compared to information about international events.

In this hypothesis there are several variables: "topic" (personal financial information vs. information about international events), "likelihood of selecting the Internet as a source," "likelihood of selecting magazines as a source," "likelihood of selecting people as a source," "likelihood of selecting TV as a source," "likelihood of selecting newspapers as a source" and "likelihood of selecting radio as a source." But which is the IV and which is the DV? Think about what's causing what. It's changing the topic that changes the sources people select, so the "topic" is the IV and the others variables are DVs. Notice that you can include more than two variables in a hypothesis; i.e., there can be multiple IVs or DVs.

RESEARCH QUESTIONS

A *research question* is exactly that — a question that can guide your research. Unlike a hypothesis, a research question can ask about anything as long as there is at least one variable that can be studied. You don't have to have a previous body of research — you can just ask because you want to know. Thus, a RQ:

- is a question,
- is related to your needs and goals,
- contains at least one variable, and
- is amenable to research and replication.

Although a research question can be very simple and narrow, it is often more than that. It can ask about more than one variable. It can ask about relations. It can be based on previous research. It can be either descriptive or relational. Try to identify the variables and spot the descriptive vs. relational RQs in the following:

1. What are the demographics of my market?
2. Are males more likely than females to shop at outdoor recreation stores?
3. What are the factors that cause people to select one brand of house paint over another?
4. How satisfied are customers with service in my restaurant?
5. What is the image of my company?
6. What target populations (based on gender, age, and lifestyle) are most likely to buy sports equipment?

Some of the RQs contain multiple variables; others just a single one. For example, RQ1 implies several demographics — income, age, etc., while RQ4 has a single variable — "customer satisfaction."

Also notice that some of the RQs are descriptive (1, 4 and 5) while others are relational (e.g., RQ2 relates "gender" to "likelihood of shopping at outdoor recreation stores").

ARE ALL RQS AND HYPOTHESES TESTABLE?

(1) Once you give some thought to this question, the obvious answer is "no." There are many questions that cannot be answered scientifically. There are a number of reasons for this. First, it may not be possible to observe the phenomenon. For example, John Edward used to have a TV show where he claimed to communicate with the dead, but there is no method for getting inside his head to find out what really is going on.

(2) Second, the phenomenon may be too brief or unique so that there may not be any evidence available. For instance, if there is a bright streak of light in the sky that many people see in different parts of the country, but there is no debris and no radar scan available, we may never know what caused the light. We might speculate that it was a meteorite or a UFO, but without confirming evidence we won't know for sure.

(3) Third, single events are not susceptible to scientific testing. There may be lots of evidence but the event cannot be observed multiple times. In other words, if it doesn't happen often enough so we can observe it many times, we can't know much about it. For example, there may have been a spike in sales of yogurt on January 16, 2006, but it hasn't happened since then. You could go back and look at what might have been different about that day — the weather, news reports about the health benefits of yogurt, or a change in the price of milk — but without other spikes to compare that one to there is no way to know if the variables change together.

Similarly, many relationships are not testable because you can't find a variable in the real world. For example, trying to compare people in the United States who own TVs to those who do not is impossible because almost everyone has a TV.

(4) Fourth, random events occur. Just look at a plot of the Dow Jones Industrial Average. While there are obvious overall trends up and down over long time periods likes months, smaller time periods show erratic fluctuations that are not easily explained (despite the daily judgments of stock analysts).

With human behavior, there are many phenomena that we cannot test or observe. While we may ask people their opinions, we cannot know for sure if that's what's going on in their head. However, you'll see that we can test for relations between what people say they will do and their actual behavior. Thus, we can know if the way we measure opinion relates to behavior.

saying what one expects will please or want I hear.

CHAPTER 7

VARIABLES AND MEASURES

O nce you have focused your needs by creating research questions or hypotheses, you need to clearly define the variables contained in them. In fact, if you can't clearly define variables, you need to go back and rework your RQs or Hs. This involves more than just naming the variables. It involves coming up with clear definitions of what you mean by each variable, including how you will measure each.

THE IMPORTANCE OF VARIABLES

Understanding variables cannot be stressed enough. By defining your variables clearly and precisely you will know what kind of data the project will produce. Of course, you won't know the exact numbers (until you do the research), but you should know whether you will be analyzing percentages or means. In addition, those clear and precise definitions will allow you or others to replicate your study if necessary.

A *variable* is a simple concept in some ways. It is simply anything that *varies* or *changes*. All you need is at least two categories (such as male/female or read the newsletter/did not read the newsletter). You can also have an infinite number of responses as in "dollars of income" or different words or phrases. While simple in definition, variables are not always easy to define or recognize.

OPERATIONALIZING VARIABLES

Once you have focused your needs into RQs or Hs, you are at the point of considering various types of research to test them. But before that you need to be very specific in defining your variables. Without those definitions you won't know what methods or analyses are appropriate.

For instance, measuring average income is very different from the effect of an ad. Variables need to be translated into specific questions, scales or observations. These need to be straightforward and easy for respondents to understand. That means creating questionnaires and other measuring instruments (see Chapters 14 and 15).

Operationalization means to create a definition for a variable that can be used in research — one that relates to the research question and meets your goals. In other words, you put the variable into operation.

Let's take the following RQ: "How much money is expected to be spent on shoes in the next year?" The only variable is "expected shoe expenditure." An operational definition could be the following question in a survey:

> "How much money do you expect to spend on shoes in the next 12 months?
> $0 to $100, $101 to $200, $201 to $300, Over $300."

This obviously meets the requirements for an operational definition (assuming the goal is to obtain percentage estimates for each category). This is not the only possible definition. Wording of the question could be different and the categories could be coded differently depending on the goals of the research. If your advertiser says they need to know the average income of your target audience, then categories would not work. So you would change the question to:

> "How much money do you expect to spend on dress suits in the next 12 months?" (Write down response in dollars.)

Some variables may be much more complicated. Take the following research question: "How much news media coverage did my promotional campaign generate?" The variable, "news media coverage," can be defined many ways. In some definitions, it is a simple single variable. In others, it may turn into multiple variables. Is it:

- Total number of stories?
- Number of stories broken down by media (TV vs. radio vs. Internet, etc.)?

- Amount of coverage (time or lineage) broken down by media?
- Amount of increase in coverage after vs. before the campaign?
- Broken down by time period (one week after, two weeks after, three weeks after) to observe when increases and drop offs occur?

Notice there are multiple variables in the definition below: total number of stories for all media, number of stories in TV, number of stories in daily paper, etc.

> Monitor all local media for the four weeks following the start of the campaign *Define within an area.*
> (record TV and radio, collect papers, download local news Web pages, etc.).
> Count the number of stories in each medium (daily paper, weekly paper, local
> magazine, radio news, TV news, local Internet) using two coders. Compile the
> number of stories for each medium and also record the total number of stories
> for all media.

Operationalizations often need a *time parameter* to be useful. Without it a respondent may be confused yet still give an answer. If the operationalization above had no time parameter, then you and others would not know the meaning of results. If a report said "There were 17 stories in local TV newscasts," does that mean in one week or six months or forever?

Even more complex are variables about opinions and attitudes that are usually measured as a scale (see Chapter 15). An operational definition for a scale might be:

> Give employees the "20-item trust scale" ("I believe the company newsletter,"
> "I cannot believe what management tells me," etc.) using a five-item response
> (strongly agree, agree, neutral, disagree, strongly disagree). Code the responses
> 1 to 5 so that "5" means more trust, and sum the responses for a scale score so
> that higher numbers mean more trust.

As long as you know what variables are in your Hs or RQs, have very specific and clear operationalizations and are confident that those operationalizations will produce the types of numbers or words that can be used to achieve your goals, then you can proceed to the methods to collect those data. You need to be very clear in your own mind, not just in the words of a definition. The rest of this chapter covers the specifics of measurement and some of the pitfalls.

MEASUREMENT

Measurement is how you plan to categorize, number, or otherwise code the observations you make for each variable. While this sounds esoteric, it is usually simple. Are you going to make a record of words, or numbers, or categories? The importance of this is that what you decide determines what kind of analysis you can do. For example, if you have categories you will probably end up with percentages, but if you have real numbers you will do means (averages), and if you have words you could just list them.

Your operationalization will determine how you write questions and responses. Clearly, there are many different styles you can use, but they should relate back to your problem statement. For example, if you were an account executive for a TV station, you might need to know "income" as actual dollars because your advertisers want to know the average income of your audience to make sure your programming fits their target. It is equally possible that they just want to know what percentage of households in your audience have annual incomes over $75,000. In the former you would need to ask real dollar amount, but in the latter you would only need to ask in categories. The following shows two ways to measure income. The first is in real numbers and the second is in categories.

> Please write down your annual household income from all sources:
> $_____

> What is your annual household income from all sources? (CHECK ONE)
> ☐ $0 to $15,000
> ☐ $15,001 to $30,000
> ☐ $30,001 or more

Here is another example of the two ways to measure a variable — this time using campaign recall. In this telephone questionnaire example, two questions are used to measure one variable. The first question screens for whether the person saw the ad, and the second elicits what they remember if they saw it. Question 1 is categories, question 2 is in real numbers (note "TOTAL").

> 1. Please tell me whether you saw any television advertising for XYZ Company in the last week.
> ☐ YES, SAW ADVERTISING
> ☐ NO, DID NOT SEE ADVERTISING/DON'T KNOW

> 2. IF YES: What do you remember from the advertising you saw for XYZ Company? [WRITE DOWN EXACT COMMENTS]
> _____
> TOTAL NUMBER OF ITEMS REMEMBERED:_____
> (NO/DON'T KNOW TO QUESTION ONE=0)

If your operationalization seeks only to measure whether people saw the ad, then the first question alone would elicit that information. However, if your operationalization defines the variable as the "number of items people remember," then you would use both questions and compute a total for each respondent.

MUTUALLY EXCLUSIVE & EXHAUSTIVE VARIABLES

When creating responses, make sure you don't have any overlap and that all possible categories are represented. Being *mutually exclusive* means that responses can't fit into more than one category — i.e., they don't overlap. The following example is not mutually exclusive. You would not use the following categories for income because there is overlap. Would "$20,000" be low or medium? In other words, the categories are *not* mutually exclusive.

☐ $0 to $20,000 (low)
☐ $20,000 to $30,000 (medium)
☐ over $30,000 (high)

Being *exhaustive* means that all possible responses are covered. The following example is *not* exhaustive. You would not use the following categories because they do not "exhaust" the possible responses; e.g., where would you check off "$75,000"?

☐ $0 to $20,000 (low)
☐ $20,001 to $30,000 (medium)
☐ $30,001 to $40,000 (high)

So far we have only looked at categories vs. real numbers. Statisticians use a more precise division that can be useful when using rank-order, scales and advanced analyses. The following section describes that system.

TRADITIONAL LEVELS OF MEASUREMENT

Levels of measurement refers to a system for determining if the measure is at the "level" that is required by your operationalization. Additionally, the level determines what analysis you can do along with what statistical tests and other estimates you can carry out. The system moves from "categories" to "ordered categories" to "arithmetic intervals" to "real numbers." These levels are named nominal, ordinal, interval and ratio. Nominal is considered "lowest" or least precise,

Table 7.1
EXAMPLES OF FOUR LEVELS OF MEASUREMENT

Nominal	Ordinal	Interval	Ratio
Male/Female	High/low/medium	IQ	Number of hours
Religious Affiliation	Positive, neutral, negative	Temperature	Number of technologies owned
Occupation	Good/fair/ poor	On a scale of 1 to 10	Expected $ spent on shoes next year
Words/phrases	Top/middle/ bottom		Age

and the levels increase in precision until reaching ratio. Examples are in Table 7.1.

> *Nominal* is two or more response categories with qualitative, not quantitative, differences. Typical nominal variable include gender (male/female), job title and religious affiliation (Protestant, Catholic, Jewish, Muslim, etc.).
> *Ordinal* is two or more responses categories that can be rank ordered. Common ordinal variables include intent to purchase a product (low, medium, or high) and attitude toward a product or service (positive, neutral, negative).
> *Interval* is responses that have equal intervals between the responses. This is similar to ratio level, but there is no real "0." IQ and temperature are two examples. Many scales are interval level of measurement (see Chapter 15).
> *Ratio* is responses with equal intervals, plus the "0" response actually means "none." There are a lot of ratio level variables. Age, time spent watching TV, are examples. An amount is usually ratio, such as dollars spent on suits in the previous year or the number of items remembered from an ad.

APPLIED RESEARCH AND LEVELS OF MEASUREMENT

While academicians pay attention to four levels of measurement because they extensively use advanced statistics, most managers and professionals are simply

Table 7.2
EXAMPLE OF DESCRIPTIVE TABLE

Table A: Rating of Factor Importance for Choosing a Hospital

	Average rating
Has the latest technology	XX.X
Has qualified physicians	XX.X
Nurses are competent	XX.X
They are friendly	XX.X

concerned with percentages or averages. They need answers to practical questions like, "What is the average income of my target audience?" or "Who attends concerts more often, males or females?" So they are only concerned with whether the measurement is categorical or numerical.

If you look at the levels of measurement in Table 7.1 you will see that there are two levels for which you have categorical responses — nominal and ordinal — and two for which there are responses with equal intervals — interval and ratio. For most industry applications, then, there are only two types of measures for variables: categorical (nominal and ordinal) and numerical (interval and ratio).

LEVELS OF MEASUREMENT AND ANALYSIS

Once you have operationalized and know your levels of measurement, you should know what analysis to expect. You'll know if you will be calculating percentages or averages to describe the results for each variable. Later, in Chapters 23 and 24, you will learn that the relational and statistical tests you perform also depend on the levels of measurement. Thus, you should be able to create tentative tables to display the results.

For example, if your RQ is "What are the reasons people use in selecting which hospital to go to?" and you use a list of reasons with hospital users evaluating each factor on a scale of one (lowest) to ten (highest importance), you know that the level of measurement is "interval," and you will be calculating averages. Thus, you can make a descriptive table that would look like Table 7.2.

The relational example in Table 7.3 is similar to Table 7.2 except that the RQ

Table 7.3
EXAMPLE OF RELATIONAL TABLE

Table B: Relation of Factor Importance to Geographic Area

	Central city	Near-Suburb	Far-Suburb
Has the latest technology	XX.X	XX.X	XX.X
Has qualified physicians	XX.X	XX.X	XX.X
Nurses are competent	XX.X	XX.X	XX.X
They are friendly	XX.X	XX.X	XX.X

asks about comparing factors among the three geographic areas based on the RQ: "Does the importance of factors for selecting a hospital vary between the central city and its two suburbs?" You would have an average for each geographic area.

GOOD OPERATIONALIZATIONS

There is no perfect or best operationalization. Many definitions and many measures can be used. But if you can't create an operational definition for a variable that someone else can understand well enough to use in another study, then your variable should not be used. Realize that many operationalizations may be appropriate for your goals. The ultimate operationalization is the question or observation along with measures that is used in a survey or other study. The test of the quality of that operationalization is whether it works in your pre-test and final study.

POOR OPERATIONALIZATIONS

Without good operationalizations, your study will make no sense to you or to others. Poorly defined variables lead to poorly constructed questionnaires and poorly designed studies. Consequently, the results of such studies are highly questionable, and decisions based on those results can leave you with unfulfilled goals. The following examples of poor operationalizations come from an internal communication study conducted where I was once employed. These examples are taken from that questionnaire, but the name of the company has been deleted.

How frequently, occasionally, or rarely do you listen to the radio?

☐ Frequently   ☐ Occasionally   ☐ Rarely   ☐ Never   ☐ Don't know

The categories above are too vague to be useful in most studies, because there is no time parameter and distinguishing between the categories can be difficult. Try to imagine how you would use the results. If 45 percent of employees checked "frequently" how could that be useful? A better way is to ask respondents the actual amount of time they spend listening to the radio (e.g., in minutes or hours of use on an average day or previous day).

Here's another example of poor operationalization.

What form of communication among the different segments of [name of organization]'s employees would you prefer?

☐ Vertical, upward
☐ Vertical, downward
☐ Horizontal, one-way
☐ Horizontal, two-way
☐ Vertical and horizontal, both ways
☐ Informal, unstructured
☐ Formal, structured
☐ Both formal & informal, unstructured & structured, both ways
☐ Don't know
☐ No response

Even with a background in research I could not figure out what the categories meant in this question. I can't even think of a revision that would make this a useful question.

Here's another question with problems.

How well run is [name of organization] in your opinion? That is, do you think it is run on a sound business basis?

☐ Fairly well run
☐ Very well run
☐ Run fairly well in some ways but not in others
☐ Don't know
☐ No response

The above question is both confusing and extremely biased. The confusion arises because it contains two different questions. Which question should I answer? The second question seems to require a "yes" or "no," but the responses seem to relate to the first part. The bias arises because the responses available do not include negative options such as "not well run." Consequently, the report might say, "There were no negative responses to how well [name of organization] is run on a business basis." At best, such a conclusion is erroneous. At worst, the organization wrote this question deliberately to obtain a false conclusion that could then be reported to its board of directors.

CHAPTER 8

VALIDITY AND RELIABILITY

Once you have operationalized your variables, you will need to take a hard look at whether your definitions "make sense." In the research world we call this examining *validity* and *reliability*. This examination, before pre-testing, can help you verify whether your operationalizations are usable. Then, gathering data about your variables during pre-testing will give you further evidence about the validity and reliability of your operationalizations.

In simplest terms, *validity* is whether you are measuring what you think you're measuring. Clearly, asking a question about income is presumed to measure income, not social status; using a scale to measure perceived image of a company should measure image, not purchase behavior.

Reliability is whether your measures will produce the same results regardless of the location or time of your study (assuming location and time are not variables in your study). You should get the same answer if you ask a person's age in their home or on the street; you should get the same answer if you ask a person's age this morning or this evening. If you get different answers, then the measure is said not to be reliable.

While the discussion that follows may seem esoteric, it is important to understand these concepts if you want accurate and usable research. Your ability to make better operationalizations depends upon having both valid and reliable measures.

TYPES OF VALIDITY

There are many types of validity, but they all focus on how successful you have been in operationalizing your variables.

Think about what might be valid and invalid ways to define variables. You might argue that asking people to tell you whether or not they like "contemporary hit radio" music is not valid because most people don't define "contemporary hit radio" the same as broadcasters. Conversely, you might argue that asking people whether or not they like "country & western" music is valid because most people define "country & western" the same as broadcasters. You may or may not be right, but this is what we mean by assess the validity of variables or measures.

Face validity means that, intuitively, the question or response categories (your operationalization) appears to measure what it is supposed to measure. It has, in other words, face value.

Predictive validity is how well the variable predicts behavior. This is not just finding relations, but it is an assertion about whether the variable is capable of being used to predict relations.

Construct validity means that the measures have been constructed well. Usually this means that the variable's definition has been used successfully in previous research or is based on good theory. This concept lays a basis for replication of research since many researchers are using the same definition for a variable so that results can be compared. For example, since the 1950s the "Roper question" has been used to identify information sources: "Where do you get most of your news about what's going on in the world today?" This question has been used for hundreds of studies and to compare results from those studies.

Content validity is how much your variable matches the concept you're really trying to measure. Sometimes your definition will be too narrow and you will have to rewrite your operationalization or you may need to ask more questions or use a scale. You often need experts to determine if your measure is appropriate. For example, if you wanted to assess how well employees understand the legal policies associated with their job, you might have an attorney look over your items or questions to make sure you have covered the appropriate legal areas correctly.

Researchers have proposed other forms of validity, and sometimes they group or name these concepts differently, such as combining content and face validity, but the important thing to remember is to go through a process whereby you are initially skeptical of your operationalization. You become less skeptical once you have considered face, construct and other validity.

Internal Validity

Internal validity is the extent to which the results of research can be related to the variables that were used. In other words, is there a link between the variables and the results or has something else caused the results? It does not refer to arguments about the usability of the variables like those in the previous section. Rather it focuses on factors during the research that can affect the study itself. Researchers have discovered many factors that can interfere with the validity of the study, including history, maturation, testing, instrumentation, regression, mortality and selection bias.

History

Has something happened during the study to alter the results? Suppose you were assessing the relation between the image of your bank and people's interest in using your bank's brokerage services, but halfway through the week of the study there was a major stock market crash. You might expect their responses would be different just because of the crash. If there were a natural disaster you might expect people to alter their shopping behavior. Remember how "Y2K" caused some people to purchase electrical generators and other survival equipment? You should pay special attention to news and events, especially disasters, that may influence responses or behavior.

Maturation

This refers to the passage of time during the study. People get older. People get tired. This can be a special problem for longitudinal research. If you were evaluating the impact of your promotional campaign that attempted to get people to exercise more, week one may show an increase, but weeks two to four might exhibit no change in activity simply due to people reaching a plateau, not a failure in your campaign.

Testing

This is the effect of participating in a study. Think about how you change when you take a test as opposed to showing up for lecture. This can be a particular problem when looking at trends or when using a pre-test/post-test experimental design. Think back to the last election for your local school board. Imagine that you were surveyed about what you thought about the candidates. Just the act of asking you questions would sensitize you to the topic, and you might pay more attention to news coverage of the candidates. Then, the next survey would find you an informed voter when you wouldn't be otherwise.

INSTRUMENTATION

This refers to changes in a response that occur because of changes in the instrument or the observer. For example, if an interviewer is sick the second day of a study, she or he may ask questions differently than on other days. If the cards that list scale items for a personal interview get sticky through handling, then people may respond differently to "icky" items.

REGRESSION

This is a statistical "law" that extreme positions tend to move toward the average of the group. Consider a campaign that tries to get people who use the least amount of toothpaste to use more. When surveyed a second time, those who are on the extreme ends of usage (both high and low users) will actually tend to move toward the mean (be less extreme). This means that if you survey just low users, you may incorrectly conclude that an advertising campaign is responsible for increased usage of your product when, in fact, there has been no effect. You need to measure the entire population to control for this problem.

MORTALITY

This refers to the drop out rate of participatants. This is more likely to affect longitudinal studies and experiments. Literally, people could die. But there are other reasons for people to drop out of your study: lack of interest, boredom or inconvenience. Imagine if all the subjects in your study were just those who had the most interest in your topic. Your study would be biased because those with less interest would be unrepresented.

SELECTION BIAS

This is the overrepresentation of a particular part of the population. If you place a questionnaire about healthcare issues on the Internet and allow anyone to fill it out as they wish, then you will end up with responses from only those who have Internet access. If you make phone calls only between 6 p.m. and 9 p.m. then you will miss evening shift workers. If you only use English in your mailing, then you potentially miss a large part of the Hispanic population.

There are other possible internal validity factors, but those above should impress upon you the importance that you need to pay to this matter.

RELIABILITY

To understand *reliability* think of what it means to be reliable. You are a consistently responsible person whether it's today or tomorrow or next week, whether you are at home, at school or at work. What you do is predictable. That should be the same for variables. Variables should consistently measure people's behavior, media habits, opinions and so forth. In other words, you would get a similar answer whether you asked a person inside a building, on the street, this morning or tonight.

Unlike validity, which relies primarily on argument, reliability can be quantitatively assessed, and there are many statistics to do that. Reliability looks at how consistent measures are from observer to observer, internally, over time or from one version to another.

Inter-observer reliability evaluates the consistency between observers using coders (raters or people who assign categories to words) and is especially useful for "content analyses." If you wanted to know how positive news coverage was for your company, you might examine all newspaper articles that mentioned your company name. Some coders might interpret an article as "very positive" while others would say "lukewarm," and so on. It is important that the coders use the same meaning for "positive," "negative," "neutral," etc. You can use a statistic called "intercoder reliability" to correlate their work to test how closely they agree on meanings.

Internal consistency is often used on scales and other multi-item measures. Frequently a "split-half" test is done, comparing odd items with even items. A correlation between the two halves should be very high. Statistics like "alpha," "inter-item correlation" and "item-total correlation" compare how well individual items correlate with the total score on the scale.

Stability (also called *test-retest reliability*) assesses how consistent responses are over time with the same or similar populations. Statistics like correlations are used to estimate how well tests, scales and questionnaires relate across different time periods.

Cross-test reliability (also called *parallel forms*) takes a large number of items and splits them randomly into two halves. Each half is administered separately with the expectation that the two separate tests are highly correlated. Imagine a professor has generated 100 multiple-choice questions for an exam. If the professor randomly selected 50 for each test, and then half of a class got Test A and the other half Test B, you would expect the correlation between scores on the two tests to be very high if the test was reliable.

(A similar test is used for scales whereby a random selection of half the items in the scale is compared with the other half. This is called *split-half reliability.*)

Obviously, reliability is best tested statistically when there are multiple items to compare, as with scales, but even individual questions can be examined for reliability over time and space. As is the case with validity, you do not have to be an expert at reliability statistics to recognize reliability problems. If you ask a question during a pre-test and you get vastly different responses for no reason, then you might suspect reliability problems.

EXTERNAL VALIDITY

External validity deals with factors outside your study. These factors affect the ability to generalize to the population from which the sample was selected. External validity examines the extent to which inferences can be made and to whom they can be made. This is important because you must know the limits of your study. Going too far, making imprecise predictions, can lead you to make bad decisions. For instance, if you drew a sample from Albany, New York, you cannot expect it to represent all people in New York State or the United States in general.

External validity is an examination of what can affect *representativeness*; that is, how close does the sample match characteristics of the population in your study. It assesses the factors causing participant bias or problems with the sample.

Reactive effects occur when people's responses or behaviors change because they are sensitized by the research itself. They could change just because they know they are being observed or because they start thinking about a topic they wouldn't normally consider. For instance, if you were conducting surveys with the same people over time and asked questions about Coke vs. Pepsi, you have to wonder if they pay more attention to the taste of their drinks now than they previously did.

Selection biases can occur when people volunteer to participate or you have selected participants that do not reflect or represent the overall population. In experiments if you do not randomly assign subjects to treatments, you run the risk

JOEY REAGAN

of people choosing the treatment they like or seems more fun. If you were testing the effect of humorous vs. serious ads and you let people select which one they watched, you might get only serious people viewing the serious ad. Then the effect of the experiment would be caused by the subjects' feelings rather than the ads themselves.

ACCURACY & PRECISION

Two other concepts deserve attention. *Accuracy* refers to the relative amount of error in your research. Think of shooting a rifle at a target: the rifle is your definition of your variable and the target is what you're trying to measure. You want to hit as close to the bull's eye as possible. Errors can arise in many areas. Problems with validity and reliability are just two examples. There is random error associated with selecting samples, and you can calculate how much that error is (see Chapter 20).

Precision is related to accuracy, but it refers to how general or specific the definition of your variable is. Being precise — being more specific — helps you be more accurate. As an example, think about measuring people's attitudes. You could ask one question, but several questions would help you better measure the many dimensions of attitudes.

Precision also relates to the number of responses people can select from. For example, you can ask respondents to "agree or disagree," but allowing a five-point response — "strongly agree, agree, neutral, disagree, strongly disagree" — will allow you to more precisely differentiate subgroups of attitude. A more precise measure would be to ask people to rate "on a scale of 0 percent to 100 percent, where zero percent is no agreement at all and 100 percent is total agreement." However, sometimes people do not or cannot make such fine distinctions and a five-point scale may be accurate enough to meet your research needs.

CONTROLLING VALIDITY AND RELIABILITY PROBLEMS

Obviously, you want to eliminate validity and reliability problems. If you cannot eliminate them, you would like to account for them. So the more control you have over them the better off you are. Experiments can be designed to either control for or account for them as you will see in Chapter 11. When you cannot do an experiment, you will need to assess the impact of these factors on your study.

Specific designs have specific problems. In nonexperiments it is almost impossible to control external factors. You will have to pay attention to these issues.

Random sampling is one way to control or eliminate some problems, especially selection bias (see Chapters 18 and 19). When doing panel studies you are especially susceptible to the "testing" impact. So you either have to assume the impact is slight or you might design a companion Trend Study to see if there is an impact.

CHAPTER 9

RELATIONS AND CAUSE & EFFECT

N ow that you have an understanding of the basic concepts for starting a research project — needs, hypotheses and research questions, and defining your variables — it is time to examine two other important concepts.

The first is the *relation* between variables. This is important because that is a top goal of most research. Simple descriptions can tell you something about your audience or market. For example, knowing the average income can help you determine whether your market can afford your service. But knowing if people with higher incomes are more likely to seek your service would be helpful in selecting target audiences, determining appropriate media buys and designing effective campaigns.

Assessing *cause-and-effect* is even better than simply knowing if a relation exists because you can be more confident in predicting how people will behave. For example, you may find a relation — such as employees who read your company newsletter also have a more favorable opinion of management vs. those who don't read it — but it's possible that newsletter reading may not have *caused* that opinion. It may be just as likely that the opposite is true, that the favorable opinion of management caused people to read the newsletter. Knowing which variable is the cause and which is the effect will help you determine whether it's worth expending company resources on the newsletter and campaign to get employees to read it.

There are times, however, when it is impossible to determine cause-and-effect. For example, you will see in Chapter 11 that random assignment is essential in experiments to determine cause-and-effect, but you can't randomly assign income in an experiment. The most you can know is that there is a relation by observing differences between different income levels. In such situations you will have to rely on the relation as the best evidence for inferring cause-and-effect.

RELATIONS

A *relation* requires two or more variables changing together — as one of the variables changes, so does the other variable. There are many examples. There is a relation between education and income — as education increases so does income. There is a relation between television viewing and academic grades — as TV viewing increases, grade-point average decreases. There is a relation between gender and technology adoption — males are more likely to adopt new technologies than females. Then there are relations we would *like* to find, such as the one between an advertising campaign and actual sales (i.e., as attention to the advertising increases, sales increase).

Researchers are careful to distinguish between different types of relations because we are not just interested in change but *how* things change: do they go up together, down together or opposite each other? Researchers have the following specific terms for these relations:

> *Positive relation.* As the values of one variable increase, the values of the other also increase. For example, as the years of education increase, income also increases. Researchers would say, "Education is positively related to income."

> *Negative relation.* As the values of one variable increase, the values of the other decrease. For example, as the hours of TV viewing per day increase, the minutes spent reading newspapers decrease. Researchers would say, "TV viewing is negatively related to newspaper reading."

> *No relation.* As the values of one variable increase, the values of the other stay the same or change randomly. For example, as a person's intelligence (IQ) increases, height changes randomly. Researchers would say, "There is no relation between IQ and height."

Of course, you can't have positive or negative relations when one or more of the variables has no order, such as gender (gender cannot increase or decrease; you cannot have more or less gender). With these variables you either have or do not have a relation as exemplified by the following.

Relation. As the values (categories) of one variable change, the values of the other also change. For example, married people are more likely to own a home than singles. Researchers would say, "There is a relation between marital status and home ownership."

No relation. As the values (categories) of one variable change, the values (categories) of the other do not change. For example, males are just as likely as females to drink espresso. Researchers would say, "There is no relation between gender and espresso consumption."

These positive and negative relations will come up again in Chapter 23's coverage of correlation.

CAUSE-AND-EFFECT

Relations have limited use for inferring cause-and-effect. All the relation tells you is whether the values of two variables rise or fall together. Cause must specify that an independent variable causes a dependent variable, not the other way around, *and* that there aren't other causes.

Consider, for example, the following relation: "Happier people are healthier people." If you interpret this to mean that being happy causes people to be healthy, then you would design a campaign to teach people how to be happy, expecting that they then would end up being healthy. But flipping that around — "Healthier people are happier people" — is just as reasonable a statement as the previous one. You then expect that being healthy causes people to be happy. In this case, you would design a campaign to teach people healthy lifestyles expecting that they would then end up happy. Without knowing which causes what, you don't know which campaign to pursue.

There are many examples of relations in which it is difficult to tell what causes what. For example, "Children who watch more violent television programs are more likely to commit crimes." Or is it, "Children who commit more crimes are more likely to watch violent television programs?" An alternative explanation is that there is another variable causing the effect; "Unsupervised children are more likely to watch violent television *and* are more likely to commit crimes than supervised children."

An important consideration for communication professionals is to determine whether a campaign caused an outcome. For example, if you are selling a product, you would certainly want to know whether (a) "People who paid more attention to my media campaign are more likely to buy my product" or (b) "People who buy my product are more likely to pay attention to my media campaign?"

So how do you know which is the cause and which is the effect in a relation? You have to show that one of the variables is the cause (the IV — independent variable) and the other variable is the effect (the DV — dependent variable). You demonstrate this by satisfying the three conditions of cause-and-effect:

1. *Time order* — one variable must precede another in time.
2. *Relationship* — the two variables are statistically related or correlated.
3. *Elimination of other causes* — the IV selected is responsible for the correlation with the DV instead of other independent variables.

For *time order*, you can control when people are exposed to the independent variable (as in an experiment), or you can demonstrate logically that the one variable preceded the other. For example, it is logical that gender precedes income. We are born male or female, and changes in income usually do not change our sex.

Relationships are demonstrated by conducting a quantitative study, and usually using a test to demonstrate statistical significance which shows there is a relationship or correlation (see Chapter 24).

Elimination of other possible causes is often the most difficult because it requires controlling people and their environment. Some controls are clearly impossible. You cannot control the home environment for a telephone survey. Experiments provide the best controls, but in situations in which you cannot conduct an experiment, you can use longitudinal designs to account for other variables. If you suspect some variables might be causes then you can include them in your study and statistically account (i.e., control) for them.

Let's assume you believe that a new corporate magazine will increase morale and, thus, increase productivity of your account executives or sales staff. You assume that "before and after publishing the magazine" is the IV and the "account executive's sales volume" is the DV. Could you demonstrate cause-and-effect by comparing sales volume of one week before with two weeks after you introduced the corporate magazine (assuming sales volume increased)? Not definitively. Why not?

- Have you satisfied time order? Yes, you showed that changes in sales volume occurred after introduction of the magazine.

- Have you demonstrated a relation between communication and sales volume? Yes, assuming you found a statistical relation between your variables. As time changes (before vs. after) so did sales volume, and it is a positive relation.

- Have you eliminated other factors? No! Think of the other possible variables that can account for increases in sales volume. Did the economy get better? Did a competitor go out of business? Did changes in the weather change buying habits? If you take these variables into account and showed no relation between them and sales volume, then you have a stronger case for cause-and-effect.

Despite having problems with the impact of other factors, you can still present evidence — and sometimes the only evidence possible — by showing time-order and relation. Both are vital components of cause-and-effect. And when making decisions, use your best evidence. Just keep in mind the possibility that other factors may impact the findings.

CHAPTER 10

QUALITATIVE DESIGNS

Once you have clearly specified your needs, goals, research questions (RQs), hypotheses (Hs) and operationalizations, you are ready to consider the nature of the research design and data collection method. Keep in mind that "design" is different from "data collection technique." For example, while you may eventually do a mail survey, selecting whether to do a survey is a different consideration from choosing to do mail. That is, the design you choose (focus group, cross-sectional survey, experiment, in-depth interview, etc.) is separate from your data collection technique (mail, phone, e-mail, in-person, etc.).

Qualitative and quantitative designs are usually considered separately. This chapter covers qualitative designs. Chapters 11 and 12 cover quantitative experiments and surveys. Chapter 13 covers data collection techniques.

The term "qualitative" has slightly different meanings to different types of researchers. For example, some call a survey qualitative if it doesn't use a random sample while others call all surveys quantitative because surveys are usually used to collect numerical data. Even some marketing researchers attach a different meaning to qualitative, defining it as having "higher quality" data. The most popular definition is that *qualitative* is a study that involves collecting nonsample-based descriptive data. You'll see in the succeeding chapters that I define all surveys and experiments as "quantitative," and I require that they are based on random samples or random assignment. Thus, a "survey" that used a *convenience sample* — a form of nonrandom sampling — would not qualify as a "survey" under my definition.

Instead, I would call it a "convenience study," which will be discussed in this chapter.

Before examining qualitative designs, you should understand that there is a place for *informal* research as well as research based on the 15 steps in the *formal* research plan described in Chapter 3.

INFORMAL VS. FORMAL RESEARCH

Informal research is any attempt to gather information that is not guided by a research plan. It is timely, inexpensive and easy to conduct. You don't need any special expertise to do it, but you often get serendipitous results. Of course, it is limited to the specific interactions or information peculiar to that situation. For example, asking a consumer to read advertising copy will tell you whether there are major problems understanding the writing, but it will not tell you whether the ad appeals to your target market. Informal research includes:

- Unsolicited customer or employee comments
- Reading competitors' newspaper ads over coffee
- Reading trade publications
- Talking with colleagues
- Chatting with some employees

Informal research can be useful because it helps reduce our biases, our narrow views of the world. It makes us aware of divergent views and behaviors. It can be used quickly and easily to get opinions about things like newsletter copy or new packaging. It can reveal potential problems. By its nature, informal research is difficult to replicate. Try to imagine duplicating a research project that involves "talking to a few people on the street to get some new ideas." An example of informal research is the Red Robin customer comment card in Figure 10.1.

Formal research follows a step-by-step research plan so that it is well focused and designed to fit your needs and goals. It can be either quantitative or qualitative. What makes it formal is that it has a purpose and follows a well-defined set of procedures. It requires planning time, execution and analysis time, money and expertise. But that investment usually produces more accurate judgments of target population characteristics, behavior, attitudes, opinions and so on. Formal research includes, but is not limited to:

- Experiments
- Surveys

JOEY REAGAN

Figure 10.1
RED ROBIN CUSTOMER COMMENT CARD
(Used by permission of Red Robin International, Inc.)

WHERE ARE WE?

| #1 | #2 | #3 | #4 |
| We Let You Down. | We Were O.K. | We Were Good! | We were a WOW! |

Using the smile-meter, circle the corresponding number following each question.

Did you have fun? 1 2 3 4
Did our food satisfy your taste buds? 1 2 3 4
Did you enjoy the beverages? 1 2 3 4
We care - did it show? 1 2 3 4
Were our team members friendly? 1 2 3 4
Did you get a good value for your money? 1 2 3 4
Was our restaurant clean? 1 2 3 4
Do you like our menu selections/variety? 1 2 3 4
What did you order? _____

What would you put on the menu if you owned the joint?
_____

Comments: _____
_____
_____
_____
_____
_____

Your name: _____
Address: _____
City: _____ State: ___ Zip: _____
Phone: _____ E-mail: _____

Number of people in your party? _____

I visit Red Robin: _____First Time
_____1-2 times per month _____3-5 times per month
_____once every 2 months _____other _____

What prompted you to come to Red Robin (besides hunger!)?
___Radio ___TV ___Newspaper ___Direct Mail ___Billboard
___A Friend ___Movie-Theatre___Other _____
Day & time of visit: _____
    Server's name: _____
    Location: _____

Visit our website at www.redrobin.com

ARE WE WHERE YET?

Red Robin aspires to deliver a WOW! adventure full of fun & scrumptious, mouth-watering vittles, innovative concoctions in beverage technology & award-winning desserts. We care about YOU and how you feel when you're with us. Are we there yet? Please, take a minute and let us know!

- Focus groups
- Intercepts
- Case studies

The value of formal research is that it can be representative of your target population and involves a process that others can follow. Consequently, you are very confident that estimates you get for your target population are accurate.

Is formal research scientific? Yes. Experiments and surveys are scientific because they adhere to systematic procedures and accepted practices that have been verified through a long history of research applications in academia and in business research (see Chapter 1 on what constitutes science). The most important aspect of scientific research is that it be replicable — that is, you and others know the procedures and operationalizations of the original study well enough to be able to duplicate it in order to extend that research or confirm the original findings. This is especially useful when you want to see if people's attitudes or behavior have changed. Scientific research usually requires "representative" samples.

Most qualitative research, on the other hand, is not scientific because it is not representative of a population. For example, case studies are open to the idiosyncratic interpretation of the person reading. Those idiosyncracies are impossible to replicate. In another example, if you did two convenience studies, one at a mall and one at a university, you would get different average ages, incomes, educational levels and other characteristics, neither of which would be representative of the overall population. Nevertheless, nonscientific research is useful because it yields ideas that can stimulate creative approaches to a problem.

Regardless of whether it's formal or informal, keep in mind that unfocused research tends to be inefficient. Merely sitting in a restaurant to pick up stray comments may or may not be useful. You could sit all day and not learn anything. If, however, you first identify a potential problem with service whereby you choose to sit in a restaurant to observe service and listen for potential comments about the staff then the endeavor has purpose.

WHAT IS QUALITATIVE DESIGN?

Qualitative research tends to be exploratory in nature, and since it is not usually representative it cannot be used to infer behavior or characteristics in the target population. However, qualitative research makes up for this deficiency by eliciting depth of thought and breadth of comments and ideas.

Qualitative can be especially useful when you have no idea where to start, such as when you haven't a clue about what your employees think about your company or what your market thinks about your product. It can also be useful for developing topics for study and questionnaire items that can be used in later quantitative studies.

JOEY REAGAN

Qualitative usually refers to designs intended to elicit words rather than numbers and is almost always descriptive. That is, you cannot test whether there are relations or cause-and-effect. However, qualitative studies often suggest relations that you can test later in quantitative designs.

If your variables tend to be "open-ended" (soliciting words and comments rather than short responses) and your research questions focus on discovering ideas or you just want to know what people are saying, then you probably want to use one of the qualitative designs. As there are several to choose from, you will need to match the design to your RQs and operationalizations. For example, the following two research questions dictate very different designs.

RQ1: What do people think about when considering where to go on vacation?
       (I need some new ideas for a resort's campaign.)

RQ2: What new bakery products might people like?
       (I own a single bakery in a Dallas suburb.)

In the first question, you assume people have taken vacations and already have some ideas about what they want, so you would just ask about existing ideas. For the second question, people may not have given much thought to a new bakery product. So getting them to talk about what they like and dislike, responding to what others like and dislike, and coming up with appetizing ideas would be more useful.

SMALL SAMPLE STUDIES   *Conclusions!!!*

Small sample studies are just that, small groups — usually less than 20 participants. They may be randomly selected or not, but because of the small size you cannot make accurate generalizations. Regardless, they can be useful for generating comments — e.g., hearing the language people use to describe your product and giving you new ideas. They can generate comments about anything, including your service, your competitors, your communication style and so on.

However, to be more useful, these comments need to be focused. For example, if you were developing a scale to measure the image of your television station, you might use small samples in two ways. First, you could use a small sample of about 20 people and interview them on the phone to ask, in an open-ended way, what they think about TV in general, the stations in the market, your station, the personalities in the market, etc. Second, using their phrases you could develop a "TV image scale," but you'll need to test it to make sure it works, again using a small sample.

In-Depth Interviews

In-depth interviews (sometimes called *depth interviews*) are usually conducted one-on-one — that is, one interviewer and one interviewee. They get into people's minds beyond "top-of-mind" responses. Instead of just finding out "I like it" or "It's just OK" or "They do a good job," you can probe for why people said what they did, and you can keep on probing. Those probes may produce other comments and insights that the respondent would never have mentioned without the probes. Interviews can last an hour or more and usually end when no new ideas are forthcoming. Most in-depth interviews are recorded.

This is similar to focus groups, below, but the advantage is that each individual is free to say what they want without being interrupted and without having to expose their comments to scrutiny and judgment from other people. They can speak more frankly about sensitive topics.

Doing in-depth interviews requires formal preparation — identifying problems and writing an initial set of relevant questions to begin the interview. Data collection is achieved by asking the participant a couple of questions and then letting the answers guide the discussion. It is important that interviewer biases are kept in check by letting the participant guide the discussion. Normally a small number of interviews is done, from two to seven.

Analysis is difficult because each interview is unique. Usually you receive a transcript or recording to review. Since the purpose is exploratory, you look for ideas or comments you haven't heard before, such as, "I just don't trust filling out the company's parking sticker form" or "I'm embarrassed buying adult diapers."

How do you get people to participate? If it's a homogeneous group, like a business association or set of employees, then a small random sample can be drawn from a list of members or employees. If it's a general population study, you can draw a sample of telephone numbers (see Chapters 18 and 19 for sampling). Usually you will offer an incentive to get people to participate, such as a couple of hours off work for employees or a monetary inducement (as high as $100 or more for a general population study). In-depth interviews can be especially useful for talking about delicate subjects like:

- Adult diapers
- Employee comments about the department head
- Extreme political issues
- Relatives
- Medical issues
- Sexual habits

CONVENIENCE STUDIES

If you interview people simply because they appear at a convenient location, it is called a *convenience study*. This includes meeting halls, community centers, work sites, shopping malls ("mall intercept"), or schools. Electronic locations are also used through Internet sites and bulk e-mail lists.

The apparent advantage of these studies is that large numbers of people can be interviewed quickly at very low cost. However, the lack of representativeness of these groups to a larger population makes them suspect if used as a substitute for a scientific survey. You could interview 300 or more people in just a few hours, but those interviews often will represent a narrow group of people, not the general population. For example, if the interviews are collected at a shopping mall, people who don't shop at that mall never get interviewed; if at a community center, people without a special interest in community activities will be unrepresented.

The advantage of the convenience sample is that you can do quick and inexpensive explorations of ideas, messages or visuals (print ads, videos, packaging and the like). For example, you could do some initial testing of product packaging. Suppose you created a new type of wood sealant along with an artist's mock-ups of several package styles that were pasted on the outside of the cans. Intercepting people at a mall, you could recruit them to view each mock-up. They could answer recall questions about the brand, pictures and copy, and make other comments. If there were problems understanding the wording or with other aspects of the packaging, you could rework your mock-ups and test again.

Suppose you wanted to taste test a new food product. Often a concern is that the new product taste is substitutable for its competition. Obviously, personal interviews with a large random sample are too expensive, so you could use convenient locations where people eat or buy the product.

Remember, even with a large number of interviews, convenience studies are not representative and cannot be used to estimate behavior, attitudes or perceptions in the general population, and they cannot be used to estimate things like sales and changes in image.

CASE STUDIES

A *case study* is exactly what it says — examining a case or example to get ideas. But you do not casually stroll through cases to generate ideas. You formulate a problem statement and make a search for relevant cases that may provide insight into your problem.

The difficulty might be in finding relevant cases. Business and academic associations and some business journals publish case studies. Associations often provide cases in print and now in a search mode on the Internet. For example, the International Association of Business Communicators publishes the annual "Gold Quill Winning Workplans." If you were a member you could access hundreds of cases.

Suppose you work for a property development company that is in the unenviable position of having to move elderly tenants out of their homes to make way for new construction. You would like to prepare yourself with ideas to deal with media should some tenants balk at moving. You'd like to find cases from others who have dealt with similar problems. I tried the following online. Of course, future searches may produce different results.

- Find a search engine: www.google.com.
- Enter keywords: elderly tenants "negative publicity" case study.
- First ten hits produce nine case studies of negative publicity.
- One hit, "Handling a Media Crisis," exactly matches negative publicity associated with the eviction of elderly tenants.

AN INTRODUCTION TO FOCUS GROUPS

Focus groups are what the phrase implies: groups in a dialogue or discussion that move from a general discussion of a topic to a focused discussion of that topic. Important also is to move from what an individual can think up on her own to how individuals react to each others' comments and ideas. Focus groups are very structured, leading the participants through a set of more and more focused questions or topics. They are similar to in-depth interviews in that the purpose is to probe deeper thoughts. You would like to draw out the breadth of the thoughts and the meaning behind the thoughts.

You will have to recruit participants, often offering a monetary incentive. The sizes of focus groups range from as few as seven to as many as 20. Too few means not enough interaction; too many means an uncontrollable mob and not enough time for all to express themselves.

Focus groups need to have structure and control because the group can get off track or a few individuals can dominate the conversation. You will need a moderator (also called monitor or facilitator) who knows how to control the group, when to follow-up important comments, when to close the discussion and move to another question, and when to deviate from the agenda.

You will need to find a room. Many data collection facilities have a focus

Table 10.1
EXAMPLE OF FOCUS GROUP AGENDA

Focus Group Agenda: Participation in Banking Investment Programs

I. Introduction, purpose of the gathering. Screening questionnaires can be filled out at this time. Warm up questions. (Develop commonality of the group.)
  A. Do you have kids? Ages?
  B. What's your favorite ice cream?
  C. Future desires for yourself/kids/retirement?

II. Start discussion
  A. What kind of bank accounts do you have? Why?
  B. What banks do you use/not use? Why/why not?
  C. How is the service? Getting better? Worse? Why?
  D. Other services you'd like to see? Why?

III. Transitions
  A. Do you have stocks? Bonds? Through a broker?
  B. Do you have retirement plans?
  C. Have you heard of using your local bank to buy stocks? Do you do that?
    Would you? Why/why not?

IV. The real focus
  A. Have you heard of XYZ bank?
  B. What do you think of XYZ bank?
  C. Did you know that they have investment services? How did you hear about it?
  D. Would you use XYZ bank for your investments? Why/why not?

group room with one-way mirrors so you can observe and video record the group. Many local research companies have a focus group room. These facilities are already set up to record the discussions. Because nontextual cues (facial expressions, body movements, etc.) are important, observers should take notes so that scowls, bitterness in the voice and other cues can be associated with the transcript of the interviews.

Focus groups are good for generating ideas and are especially useful for getting the actual language people use to describe your topic. They can be particularly helpful for coming up with wording for questionnaires or scales to be used in a future study. They can also provide language to be used in your promotion or advertising copy.

Since control and structure are important, an agenda is mandatory to help the moderator lead the group to the focus. Note that the agenda example in Table 10.1 is not just a list of topics to discuss but is a plan to lead participants from a general

Figure 10.2
PROJECTION TECHNIQUE FOR PET FOOD
(Used by permission of Phoebe Reagan)

discussion to the specific issue you want information about.

How do you make up focus group questions? Where do the ideas come from? These can be created, in part, just by asking your client and yourself what you want to know. In addition, other qualitative designs can help. For example, you can conduct in-depth interviews with a few employees or ask customers to fill out comment cards to generate ideas.

Discussions and verbal responses are not the only ways to generate ideas and participation. Projective techniques can trigger thoughts (see example in Figure 10.2). These can be used to break the ice and get people involved in the discussion. They can also be used privately to generate responses an individual might not make in a group setting. Projective techniques include:

- Role-playing activities (participants pretend to use the new product)
- Word association ("ABC Company"– _____ ; "fun"– _____)

- Sentence completion ("The best thing about working in this company is ...")
- Pictures, music and other nontext stimuli.

How do you analyze the comments?

Soon after the group is done you will want a transcript of the discussions. Some computer programs exist to do word searches and content analyses. Whether you content-analyze or simply read or scan the transcripts and notes, you must keep your purpose in mind. Are you looking for themes that will assist your creative campaign, language to use in a survey, or some other use? More than one person should examine the transcript so you can verify if your interpretation matches theirs. If you do content analysis, you would compute intercoder reliability to verify that interpretations are consistent.

But use care in interpreting the results. Many professional market researchers who use focus groups caution that this is the method most often misused when the results are applied to evaluation rather than the generation of ideas and messages. Remember that focus groups are not representative of any target. Thus, you cannot estimate sales or other indicators of success.

Table 10.3
CHARACTERISTICS OF QUALITATIVE AND QUANTITATIVE DESIGNS

Qualitative	Quantitative
In-depth responses	Top-of-mind responses
Unexpected results	Control of stimuli and questions
Generates ideas	Good for spotting trends
Simple organization	Good for evaluating campaigns
Inexpensive	Can be very expensive
Difficult to analyze	Easy analysis of numbers
Spontaneous	Not spontaneous
Not replicable	Replicable
	Good for discovering relations/causes
	Good descriptions of the market

WHICH IS BETTER, QUALITATIVE OR QUANTITATIVE?

Neither. The important issue is whether you have chosen the appropriate design for your needs, goals, RQs and Hs. The match of characteristics between your needs and the design varies. For example, simplicity is a general advantage of qualitative studies, but some qualitative designs, like focus groups, can be complex to manage and the results difficult to analyze. Table 10.3 compares the overall characteristics of qualitative and quantitative designs.

CHAPTER 11

QUANTITATIVE DESIGN: EXPERIMENTS

Q uantitative designs are usually used to collect numerical data. These include surveys or polls, experiments and most content analyses. In all of these designs, it is possible to collect nonnumerical data ("verbatims" or "open-ended" responses) that can be categorized and used quantitatively, such as the percentage of respondents making negative statements about image.

EXPERIMENTS

An *experiment* is a test of cause-and-effect with the independent variable being *treatments* or *stimuli,* and the dependent variable being some *observation* of changes in behavior, attitude, opinion, or other variable. The independent variable is assumed to be the cause; the dependent variable is assumed to be the effect. In experiments, the independent variable can be manipulated, and the dependent variable is observed.

The best test of cause-and-effect is an experiment. Since the experimental situation is tightly controlled, you can eliminate many other possible causes of the DV. In Chapter 9, you learned that cause-and-effect has three requirements. Experiments satisfy those requirements by (1) controlling the time-order by first providing the independent variable or stimulus and afterwards measuring the dependent variable or effect; (2) demonstrating a relation with statistical testing of the relation between the IV and DV; and (3) controlling external factors in two ways: controlling the environment to eliminate external variables (or to make sure the impact of them is the same for all groups) and by random assignment to prevent people's internal variables (values, attitudes, gender, etc.) from causing the outcome.

Classic experiments have an independent variable that uses treatment groups (or stimulus groups) along with a control group that does not get the treatment. Observations are then made of how participants/subjects in each of the groups responded by measuring the subjects' behavior, attitude, knowledge, etc. Each group may contain 20 or more subjects. The experiment is conducted in a "lab," usually a room or auditorium. The groups are compared and an effect is inferred if the groups are statistically different.

Lab experiments are best for controlling the environment. For example, you can control the IV by deciding how much stimulus each subject receives, such as comparing exactly zero, one, and two hours of violent TV viewing. You also control the room temperature, when the experiment takes place and other external factors.

However, there are problems with using a lab environment. It is not "real." Imagine what it is like to watch a TV commercial at home when you can leave the room to get a snack or go to the bathroom vs. watching an ad in a room where there are no distractions and you are under pressure to pay attention. Your behavior would be modified. If being "real" is very important, then *field experiments* are more appropriate. But field experiments are subject to less control and they are often difficult to create (discussed later in this chapter).

Many types of experiments are used in academic research, but true experiments are rarely used in applied communication research (industry research), because they can be difficult and expensive to set up and conduct, and recruiting subjects from the real world is usually very expensive compared with academic experiments that use students as subjects. However, applied experiments can be done if the set-up is simple.

For example, you could test several new layouts (type style, size of columns, etc.) that you are considering for your local newspaper. This is important because a major makeover should require solid evidence before risking a change. A simple experiment would use the layouts as treatments, Layout 1 vs. Layout 2 vs. Control (current layout; see Table 11.1). The observation could be a short questionnaire — administered after participants view their respective layout — that seeks opinions about the newspaper layout and respondent's likelihood of subscribing. Simple experiments like this can be conducted to test different versions of campaigns, print ads, video, news copy, and so on.

Table 11.1
SIMPLE EXPERIMENT TO TEST NEWSPAPER LAYOUT

	Group I	Group II	Control
Time$_1$	Layout 1	Layout 2	Current layout
Time$_2$	Observation	Observation	Observation

QUASI-EXPERIMENTS

There is wide use of *quasi-experiments* (called "quasi-" because they resemble experiments) due to the relative ease with which such studies can be done. You simply observe people before and after presenting a treatment but without a control group.

For example, you could gather 200 people in an auditorium, have them fill out a pre-questionnaire about intended purchase, show them a TV program with your ad embedded, and then have them fill out a post-questionnaire about intended purchase, hoping to find that their intended purchase had changed "because" of your ad. I put "because" in quotes since you can't know definitely if your ad caused the change since this is not a true experiment. This design is often used to test messages and is sometimes called an *auditorium test* because people are recruited to an auditorium or other convenient location to view and respond to a message.

Even if you have two or more groups, if you do not use random assignment it is also called "quasi-experiment." Remember that you can have internal validity problems if you don't maintain experimental control.

Besides their lower cost and simplicity, the advantage of quasi-experiments over true experiments is that they more closely represent actual human behavior. In the real world people are exposed to many messages, not just a single treatment, and they choose what to expose themselves to and, as is common in auditorium tests, people exhibit "normal" behavior such as talking during commercials. Table 11.2 shows the layout of a quasi-experiment.

EXPERIMENTAL DESIGNS

There are literally dozens of experimental designs. Most of the intricate designs are used by academic researchers, but there are several basic designs that are used

Table 11.2
A QUASI-EXPERIMENT

Time$_1$	Time$_2$	Time$_3$
Observation	Stimulus	Observation
Pre-launch survey	Campaign	Post-launch survey

extensively by both academicians and applied researchers. All require random assignment of subjects to be true experiments.

PRETEST/POST-TEST CONTROL GROUP

This is a straightforward comparison of at least one group before vs. after receiving a stimulus, along with a control group that is observed at the same time without the stimulus.

Suppose you have created two versions of a TV ad to increase awareness of your Web page. Version 1 is humorous; Version 2 is serious. You would like to know which version increases awareness of your ad the most. You test awareness (Observation$_1$ and Observation$_2$) by asking people if they have ever heard of your Web page, if they've seen it and what they remember about it. You assess effect of the ads by doing the experiment shown in Table 11.3.

First, you observe all three groups by asking about awareness of your Web page. Have they heard about it, seen it and what they remember about it. (This is the pretest.) Second, one group sees the humorous ad, one group sees the serious ad and a control group does not see either ad. Finally, you observe all three groups again with the same questions about awareness.

The value of this design is twofold. First, you can compare the groups to see if they are different. You can tell which group has the most awareness. If the control group has the most, then the ads have probably failed, but if the humorous ad has the most awareness, then it probably has the most effect. Second, you can assess how much change has occurred. That is, you can use Observation$_1$ as a "baseline" to make sure that Observation$_2$ shows an increase, and you can see how much of an increase there is.

The limitation of this design is that you "sensitize" subjects. Once you have asked about awareness, you do not know if the increase in awareness is because subjects are now aware of your Web page or because the groups that

Table 11.3
PRETEST/POST-TEST CONTROL GROUP DESIGN

	Group I	Group II	Control
Time$_1$	Observation$_1$	Observation$_1$	Observation$_1$
Time$_2$	TV ad version$_1$	TV ad version$_2$	Does not view ad
Time$_3$	Observation$_2$	Observation$_2$	Observation$_2$

saw the ads are now paying more attention than they normally would. You can't be sure the change is solely due to your ad.

POST-TEST CONTROL GROUP

This is the same as the previous design, but without the pretest (Observation$_1$). The experiment example used earlier in this chapter in Table 11.1 is such a design.

All groups, including the control, are observed at the same time only after the stimulus has been given. It does not sensitize subjects, but it also does not allow you to assess how much change occurs because of the stimulus.

SOLOMON FOUR-GROUP

This design overcomes the limitations of the previous two. It has the advantage of testing changes (Groups I and II in the example), but it controls for sensitization (Groups III and IV). In other words, you are sure the effect of your ad is due to the ad itself, not sensitization.

The disadvantage of the Solomon design is that it is more complex and more expensive, so you need a very good reason to justify the expense. Table 11.5 shows how you would lay out the experiment.

ADVANTAGES AND DISADVANTAGES OF EXPERIMENTS

Table 11.6 summarizes the major advantages and disadvantages of experiments. Experiments also have the advantage of being a quantitative study (see Table 10.3 at the end of the previous chapter).

Table 11.5
SOLOMON FOUR-GROUP DESIGN

	Group I	Group II	Group III	Group IV
$Time_1$	$Observation_1$	$Observation_1$	No observation	No observation
$Time_2$	TV ad	No TV viewing	TV ad	No TV viewing
$Time_3$	$Observation_2$	$Observation_2$	$Observation_2$	$Observation_2$

FIELD EXPERIMENTS

Field experiments take place in the environment in which you naturally encounter the stimulus, such as running an ad during a broadcast television program or trying out a display in the grocery store. The example of the newspaper layout test above could also be done in the field at convenient locations where people actually read newspapers — coffee shops, commuter trains, etc. Rather than randomly assigning people to view a layout, you would randomly assign layouts to coffee shops (each layout in one-third of the shops). In other words, a field experiment is one that is conducted in the real world instead of a lab.

Test marketing is an attempt at a field experiment using populations with similar demographics, economies, etc. The market that gets the product or message is the treatment group, and a second market that is matched to the characteristics of the treatment market serves as the control.

The advent of electronic networks offers additional opportunities to conduct field experiments. "Switched-addressable" or digital cable television systems can be used. Each cable TV household has a separate electronic identifier/address, and some cable systems can carry different programming to different households. You could send one version of your ad embedded in a regular TV program to a randomly selected half the system and a second version to the other half. Then, by conducting interviews soon after the ads were sent, you can compare recall or brand awareness or purchase intent between the two ads. A true experiment.

The Internet offers other opportunities where you can test messages such as banners, pop-ups and other ads by randomly alternating between different versions and then comparing the click-throughs.

Table 11.6
ADVANTAGES AND DISADVANTAGES OF EXPERIMENTS

Advantages	Disadvantages
Test cause-and-effect	Complex
Control of environment	Expensive
Control of stimulus	Planning time required
Control of external variables	Requires more expertise than survey

CHAPTER 12

QUANTITATIVE DESIGN: SURVEYS

E xperiments, of course, are only one part of quantitative design. Another option is to observe people at home, at work, on the street, in a more real situation without controlling the IV. If you observe everyone in a population we call it a *census*. The other major and more popular design is a *survey*.

While experiments are used extensively in academic research, surveys are also used a lot, too. Surveys comprise more than 90 percent of the quantitative research conducted in communication industries. They are used to measure broadcast ratings, political opinion, consumer behavior and communication.

CENSUS OR SURVEY?

In situations where the population is small, you would do a census. Small companies, a single class of 100 students, 50 people who live on one block in a city, or 25 ads that your competitor ran in the local newspaper over the past year would be easy and inexpensive to analyze.

But a census would not be practical for large populations, even those of a few thousand, because it costs too much or takes too much time to interview or observe everyone. So a more practical approach for a large population is to survey. While a censes has no sampling error (see Chapter 20), surveys can be done with samples that are reasonably accurate without the time and expense of a census.

A *survey* is a comprehensive examination of a population using a random sample, assessing variables for the purposes of describing or finding relations in that population. *Random* means that everyone in the population has an equal or known chance of being selected.

There are several types of surveys, depending on whether you are observing at a single point in time or over several time periods and whether you are observing people, things or content. Note that "survey" means something different to researchers than the general public. Most people would say, "I surveyed my room full of students" (which is really a census) or, "I surveyed the first three people I met" (which isn't a survey because it doesn't use a random sample). A survey is much more complex and must be well-tested and well-planned.

CROSS-SECTIONAL SURVEY

A *cross-sectional survey* is a one-time snapshot, or "cross section," of a population. Most surveys sample 200 to 2,000 respondents. Occasionally cross-sectional surveys are called "polls" or simply "surveys."

Cross-sectional surveys are useful for gathering large amounts of data and answers to many questions in a short time at relatively low cost. The major disadvantage is that responses lack depth or thoughtfulness. You can probe for more thoughtful responses, but the trade-off is you can't ask as many other questions. Most surveys are limited to about 35 to 40 questions or items. It is also difficult to infer cause-and-effect from a survey because it doesn't have the controls or treatments of an experiment. Cross-sectional surveys can be used for a large variety of informational needs, including, but not limited to:

- Describing the demographics of a market
- Assessing the image of a company
- Measuring the attitudes toward a political candidate or issue
- Ranking the importance of attributes of a product or service
- Testing relations between demographics and expected purchase behavior

LONGITUDINAL SURVEYS

A *longitudinal survey* is exactly what the word means — "over time." It's simply replicating a survey over two or more time periods and is especially useful for observing changes in a population. The most popular of the longitudinal designs are the trend study and panel study.

Table 12.1
COMPARISON OF TREND AND PANEL

	Time$_1$	Time$_2$	Time$_3$
Trend	Sample A	Sample B	Sample C
Panel	Sample A	Sample A	Sample A

Table 12.1 show the difference in samples for the major types of longitudinal designs. *Trend studies* use different samples over the time periods while *panel studies* keep the same sample (or respondents) through all time periods.

Trend studies are useful to see if change has occurred, such as before and after a campaign, or if market demographics or activities or attitudes have changed from one year to the next. Ratings research that uses diaries mailed to different samples for each sweep (i.e., time period) is an example of trend study.

Panels track changes, too, but they offer the added bonus of tracking individual changes. They are well known for their use in electronic monitoring of television viewing, using the same households hooked up to a electronic box that monitors television usage, day to day, month to month. Other examples include tracking changes in Internet site use (e.g, do people change their habits as they keep coming back to the same site?), tracking changes in health as people change lifestyles, and assessing how a campaign affects subscribership to cable services (e.g., tracking why subscribers drop out, then resubscribe).

Both panels and trend studies can detect general population changes, but only panels can detect *internal* changes that do not show up as an overall trend. Suppose you conducted a trend study and found that in 2005, 56 percent thought your brand was "trustworthy" and 44 percent thought it was "untrustworthy." In 2006 you found that 56 percent thought your brand was "trustworthy." Does that mean nothing much has changed? No. It is possible that half of the "trustworthy" group in 2005 changed to "untrustworthy" and about half of "untrustworthy" group changed to "trustworthy." The overall percentage stayed the same but a lot changed internally. This could mean that attitudes are unstable and susceptible to change by a campaign. A trend study would miss this.

Cable TV, satellite services, magazines and other subscription media have "churn," people dropping out then back into subscription. So while the overall penetration of subscribers stays the same, there may be many internal changes. Panals can be useful for determining why that churn occurs so you can try to counteract it.

Panels have the disadvantages of "dropout" and "bias." Dropouts occur when people refuse to participate at later time periods, move or can't be contacted for other reasons. Bias occurs when people learn from the first interview about the issues at hand. Then they may pay attention more than they usually would, preparing their responses for the next interview. Think about political polls. If people get sick of all the political advertising, they may lose interest in the campaign and drop out of a panel. However, when you ask people about political issues they may then start to pay more attention to the campaigns and form opinions when they otherwise wouldn't.

Panels and trends can be used for a large variety of needs when those needs involve tracking change, such as:

- Changes in expected purchase behavior before vs. after a campaign
- Changes in consumer concern when media report product recalls
- Tracking employee attitudes toward changes in company structure
- Changes in knowledge before vs. after training

Cohort studies are similar to trends and panels but are used to track changes in groups with similar life and time characteristics. The most popular is an age cohort, people born in the same era such as baby boomers and X-generationers. Other cohorts can be determined by education (e.g., college graduates from the 1990s) or experiences (e.g., Gulf War veterans). Cohort studies are especially useful for tracking changes in targets. Baby boomers, for example, are now facing retirement — a change that has implications for public policy (e.g., the need for more health services) and the consumer market (e.g., boomers are less likely to stick with one brand than younger cohorts, and they will increase demand for certain products like natural foods).

ADVANTAGES AND DISADVANTAGES

Table 12.2 summarizes some of the key advantages and disadvantages of cross-sectional and longitudinal survey designs.

CONTENT ANALYSIS

Content analysis is simply a survey (sometimes a census) of content rather than people. "Content" can be things like violent television programs, newspaper articles about your company, or competitors' print advertising.

JOEY REAGAN

Table 12.2:
SOME ADVANTAGES AND DISADVANTAGES OF
CROSS-SECTIONAL AND LONGITUDINAL DESIGNS

Cross-sectional		Longitudinal	
Advantages	Disadvantages	Advantages	Disadvantages
Cheap	Short answers	Cheap	Sensitization in panels
Simple	Top-of-mind	Simple	
Quick	Difficult to establish cause-and-effect	Assess overall changes	Changes to sample and response rate like dropout in panels
Lots of data	No control of external variables	Some cause-and-effect can be tested	Difficult to precisely establish cause-and-effect
Many variables	No control of stimuli	Account for some external variables like "time"	

It is easy to "capture" content. You simply collect each issue of a newspaper or magazine, record video and audio, download and store Internet content, and then conduct your study.

If the amount of content is small — say all issues of the metro newspaper for the last four weeks — you could reasonable do a census; that is, analyze all of the articles to find mentions of your company. If the amount of content is large, such as all national advertising in all print media for your competitors, you could conduct a survey, sampling a small percentage of the total content. For example, to see how often your company is mentioned in the trade press, you could do a cross-sectional survey using a random sample of your industry's professional Internet sites along with print trade publications. You could also conduct a trend study of content to examine whether coverage changes from this year to next. You might want to know if the amount of favorable vs. unfavorable media coverage changes dependent on seasons or holidays or other factors.

How you "code" the content can be difficult. Depending on your goals, different techniques can be used. In Chapter 22 we will examine dealing with words or verbatims. The analysis is fairly easy if a simple count is the goal, but difficulty is encountered when interpretation is needed.

CHAPTER 13

DATA-GATHERING TECHNIQUES

As noted in Chapter 10, you should keep the concept of research design distinct from data-gathering technique. It is possible, for example, to conduct a survey (a design) by phone, mail or e-mail (different data-gathering techniques).

PERSONAL INTERVIEWS

A *personal interview* (or *in-person interview*) merely means to gather information face to face. Various techniques can gather data in-person, either in groups or from individuals. You can usually gather very large amounts of data. For example, the Public Health School at the University of Michigan once conducted personal interviews with a questionnaire that was 74 pages long and contained more than 300 items. Needless to say, an interview took several hours and was expensive.

Since you are face to face, you can show pictures or demonstrate products, or you can show scale items that respondents can check off. This is generally more efficient and accurate than reading the items over the telephone. It is especially useful when people must interact with the product or interact with other people.

Personal interviews can be very time-consuming and expensive and can require more interviewing skill than other techniques. Interviewers must be trained to prevent the introduction of interviewer bias. Even simple gestures such as a nod might influence a respondent's answer.

Table 13.1
ADVANTAGES AND DISADVANTAGES OF PERSONAL INTERVIEWS

Advantages	Disadvantages
High contact and response rates	Can take several weeks to complete
Can conduct long, in-depth interviews	Expensive
Can supplement with observations	Some difficult contacts in gated communities, locked buildings, etc.
Can have respondent interact with stimuli	Complex organization, field management required
	Possible interviewer bias through expressions, gestures, comments, etc.

If representative samples are used, interviews may be spread across large geographic areas. Cost for interviewers alone can start at $20 per interview. Add in supervision and other overhead, and the data collection costs can easily exceed $50 per interview. National marketing firms often charge clients $200 or more for each in-person interview.

Clearly, you have to have a special reason to use personal interviews in order to justify the time and expense. Many studies using personal interviews manage the cost by using locations where it is convenient to find large numbers of people: malls, airplanes, community centers. Focus groups are conducted at central locations. Table 13.1 summarizes the advantages and disadvantages of personal interviews.

MAIL

Mail is another method of gathering data. It usually involves sending a paper questionnaire to a respondent. You can do that through the post office or, if you are surveying people in a company, a company's internal mail system.

The advantage of mail is that people can take time to make thoughtful responses, look up information, check off long lists or look at something. You can also reach people who are difficult to contact by phone. However, collecting data by mail runs the risk of having people throw the questionnaire away as junk. The mail technique is notorious for having very low response rates. Rates as low as 10 percent are common for general population studies that fail to employ good methods. Many researchers avoid using mail for general population studies, not only because response rates are low but because some people cannot read or write well and some people find written questions difficult to understand. However, simple mail surveys that provide a financial incentive (e.g., $1 bill) can often generate response rates higher than 50 percent even with general population surveys.

Another problem with mail is that respondents have greater difficulty clarifying a question or response. They would have to call someone, and most are not willing to do that. Collecting data by mail is best for those difficult to reach people for whom you can find an incentive to participate.

As mentioned above, incentives can play a big role in enticing participation. Usually part of the incentive is the loyalty that a participant has to a group. So mail is good for reaching members of associations, employees, interest groups and other homogeneous groups. Even if you are mailing to a homogeneous group, additional incentives and reminders are commonly used. A large body of experimental research has discovered several factors that improve response rates.

- Inducements:
  - A crisp new banknote
  - A prize (university stickers from the alumni association)
  - A future prize (foreign postage stamps after return of the questionnaire)
  - A chance (entry to win a computer upon questionnaire return)
  - Some value ("...returning the questionnaire will help the association develop goals")
- A deadline
- Not looking like junk mail (use the prettiest stamps, even on the return envelope)
- Sending a letter before the study begins and sending a reminder after receipt of the questionnaire

Recreational Equipment Incorporated (REI), a Seattle-based outdoor retailer whose members receive dividends each year, uses mail surveys of its membership (although they have recently chosen to no longer use mail in favor of electronic designs). Figure 13.1 shows a copy of a cover letter. Mail was especially appropriate for that study because REI members are scattered all over, active, difficult to reach, but homogeneous in their orientation to the outdoors and their membership in REI. The cover letter included two major incentives: value to the respondent by saying participation "will improve the experiences you have," and

Quality Outdoor Gear and Clothing Since 1938

September 1999

Dear REI Member:

My questions today have to do with the kinds of things retailers do (or don't do) that are important to you as a consumer. We hope, through your responses, to understand better what is important to you and how we can allocate resources in ways that will improve the experiences you have as an REI member and customer.

We want everyone to respond, so here's our offer: **If you are 18 years of age or older, not an REI employee and are a legal resident living in the U.S. (except Rhode Island), your completed questionnaire will serve as your entry into a contest to win one of three (3) $100 REI gift certificates. <u>Just write your name and co-op number on a blank piece of paper and return it with your completed questionnaire.</u>**

The long page may look like a lot of work, but the responses I am looking for are simple — one mark per attribute — so I hope you will stick with this long list and answer each one. When you have finished, please return these pages in the postage-paid envelope provided. We appreciate your help.

Very truly yours,

Sue Brockmann
Vice President, Marketing

RECREATIONAL EQUIPMENT, INC.

P.O. BOX 1938 • SUMNER, WA 98390-0800 • (253) 395-3780

Table 13.2

ADVANTAGES AND DISADVANTAGES OF MAIL TECHNIQUE

Advantages	Disadvantages
High contact rate	Return rates are low — requires more planning and cost
Good for homogeneous groups	Not good for general population studies
Good for difficult to reach groups	No chance to clarify questions
Can get thoughtful responses	Can take several weeks to complete
Low cost for wide geographic area	Can't control who and when completed

an inducement (a chance to win a $100 gift certificate). Table 13.2 summarizes the advantages and disadvantages of the mail technique.

PHONE

Telephone is traditionally the most popular data-gathering technique for researching general populations. Obviously, this is because it is relatively inexpensive, quick and can reach most people. A study can be completed in one night, if necessary, although calling over several evenings and afternoons improves response rates and provides a more representative slice of the population, reaching people who may not be available at night or on a particular day.

The major disadvantage of the phone survey is lack of depth of responses, because you are limited to about eight to ten minutes of interview time, and you are forced to accept short, top-of-mind responses.

Response rates in telephone surveys also have dropped over the last 40 years, although that has recently leveled off. Telephone technologies like answering machines, call blocking and caller ID have made it more difficult to reach some people. Public dislike for telemarketing (where someone is trying to sell something over the phone) also has adversely impacted legitimate surveys. The cell phone also has made it more difficult to reach respondents who have no line-based phone.

Because of these problems it is essential to obtain cooperation from people who answer the phone. The best way to do that is to be professional and to sound legitimate. Avoid sounding like a telemarketer. You have just a few moments to get

Table 13.3
ADVANTAGES AND DISADVANTAGES OF PHONE TECHNIQUE

Advantages	Disadvantages
Good response rates compared to mail	Lack of contact because of caller ID, voice mail, answering machines
Inexpensive	Dropping response rates
Quick	Usually short, top-of-mind responses
Good for general population studies	Concern about the impact of cell phones

the person to "buy in" to the interview. Short, professional, introductions are best. Interviewers need to be trained and supervised to achieve this professionalism. The following example achieves this goal. It uses the full name of the interviewer, rather than telemarketers' too-familiar first names only approach, reveals the purpose of the study and who is conducting it, and quickly moves into the first question. Most researchers try to put the interviewee at ease by saying they are not selling or asking for a donation.

> INTRODUCTION: Hello, I'm (FULL NAME OF INTERVIEWER) calling from Reagan Market Research. I'm not selling anything or asking for a donation. We're doing a study of how people feel about different foods, and I have a few questions for someone over 18 years of age. Are you over 18? (IF "NO": May I speak with someone over 18?).

Table 13.3 summarizes the advantages and disadvantages of the phone technique.

ELECTRONIC — INTERNET AND E-MAIL

Electronic data collection via the Internet through Web-based questionnaires or as questionnaires sent by e-mail are becoming very popular because of the ease and low cost of distribution. For the time it takes to set up a Web page or e-mail address book and a little publicity, you might get several hundreds or thousands of people to fill out your questionnaire, and the results are available instantly from your computer. Just like spam, you can send millions of questionnaires for the same price as sending a few.

Figure 13.2
SCREEN FROM WEB QUESTIONNAIRE
(Used by permission of Ching-Quo Wu)

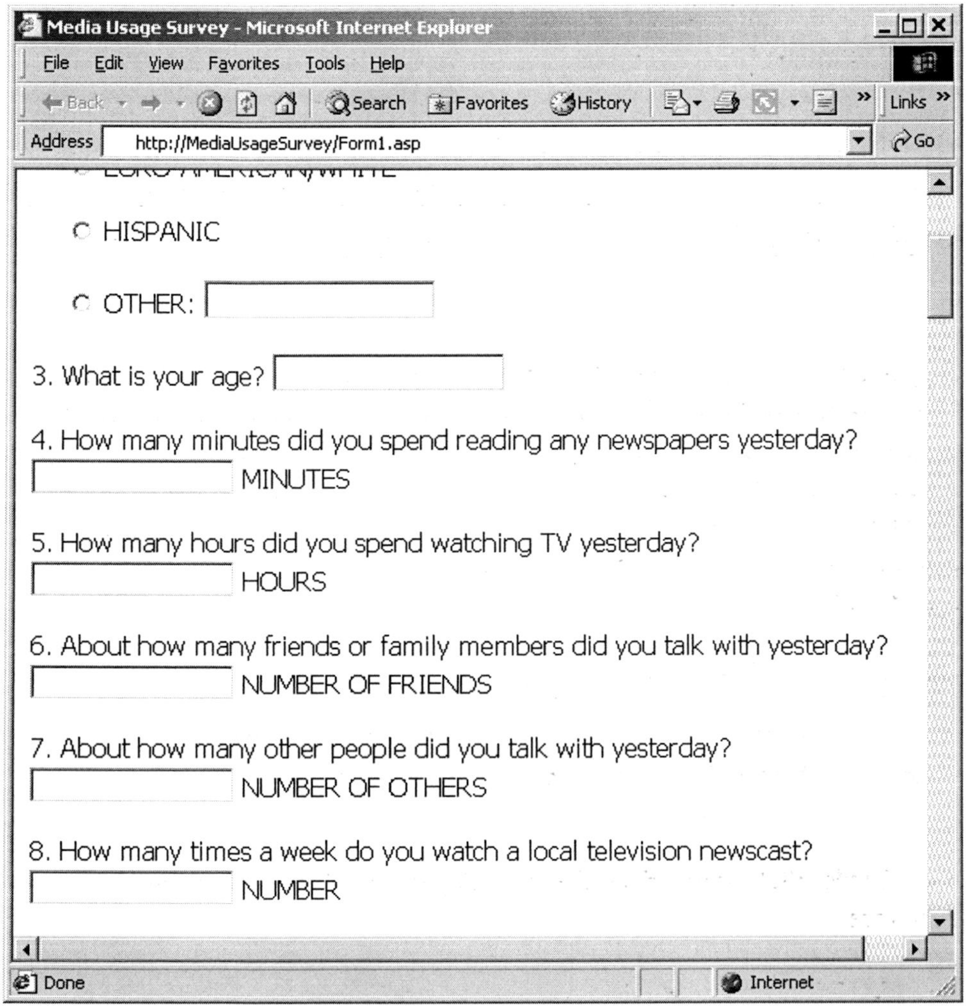

Figure 13.2 shows a screen from a Web-based questionnaire. Data can be entered directly on the screen and the computer will enter responses into a database for instant analysis.

You must be cautious because electronic techniques suffer most of the same disadvantages as mail. People often don't respond, and there's the added disadvantage that large groups of people do not have network access, whereas most

Table 13.4
ADVANTAGES AND DISADVANTAGES FOR ELECTRONIC TECHNIQUES

Advantages	Disadvantages
Very inexpensive	Similar disadvantages as mail such as low response rate
Very quick	Not good for general population studies
Immediate analysis	Limited to those with Internet access
Useful for surveys within organizations, companies, associations	Database setup can be complex, costly
	Privacy concerns

people have a postal address or phone number. E-mail should only be used for those homogeneous groups that have electronic network access and for whom you can find an incentive to participate. In addition, you have the same problems as those associated with leaving a pile of questionnaires in a public place, namely selection bias — i.e., controlling who and how the questionnaires are filled out. The advantages and disadvantages of electronic techniques are shown in Table 13.4.

Washington State University professor Don Dillman, who is internationally recognized as an expert in survey research techniques, has identified several principles to keep in mind for electronic techniques.

- Are the people filling out the questionnaire part of your target? How do you control who gets the questionnaire?
- Is there a filter in place to prevent the same person responding twice?
- Do all computers format the questionnaire correctly on the screen?
- Some people do not have the requisite browser to display the questionnaire correctly.
- Computer logic doesn't match user logic. For example, filling out a questionnaire online may use a mouse rather than a pencil.
- Motivating users may be difficult.
- "How to fill out" instructions are critical.
- Avoid distracting graphics and menus.
- Make a question and responses fit in a small screen. There is difficulty when scrolling.
- Don't expect respondents to remember instructions listed at the beginning.
- Allow respondents to proceed without inputting a response.

Table 13.5

DATABASE, UNSORTED

Name	Number of downloads, newsletter	Salary employee?	Location	Years employed	Employees supervised
Anderson,Art	16	YES	EUROPE	3	6
Bullima,Janine	14	NO	EUROPE	7	0
Fontana,Carla	0	YES	US	17	35
Honori,Della	12	NO	US	9	0
James,Leland	2	YES	US	6	26
Kuo,Zachariah	15	NO	US	5	2
Quri,Mahmu	14	NO	EUROPE	6	5
Reagan,Joey	1	YES	US	7	29
Thor,Odin	16	NO	ASIA	1	5
Wu,Ching	13	NO	US	12	0

DATABASE GENERATORS

With the advent of electronic scanners and the Internet, gathering information about the people who visit your store or Web page is practical. If your customers use checks, credit cards, smart cards, store discount cards, car rental information and other identifiers, you can create computer databases that merge data you have already collected with continuing behavior of your target population.

For employee databases, productivity can be assessed by tracking various measures like sales volume, expenses, sick days and so on. But other employment statistics (e.g., length of employment, job classification) can be combined with behavioral statistics (e.g., use of in-house communication, e-mail, Internet use) to help assess or develop communications. The example in Table 13.5 shows part of a simple database that combines usage and downloads of the in-house newsletter with several employment characteristics. Simple databases can be stored in spreadsheets and easily sorted and examined. Large "relational" databases can be used to sort through several different data files and to create subsets of those databases or new spreadsheets that combine characteristics. They are complicated

Table 13.6
DATABASE, SORTED BY DOWNLOADS

Name	Number of downloads, newsletter	Salary employee?	Location	Years employed	Employees supervised
Anderson,Art	16	YES	EUROPE	3	6
Thor,Odin	16	NO	ASIA	1	5
Kuo,Zachariah	15	NO	US	5	2
Bullima,Janine	14	NO	EUROPE	7	0
Quri,Mahmu	14	NO	EUROPE	6	5
Wu,Ching	13	NO	US	12	0
Honori,Della	12	NO	US	9	0
James,Leland	2	YES	US	6	26
Reagan,Joey	1	YES	US	7	29
Fontana,Carla	0	YES	US	17	35

and commonly require an expert to set up.

Table 13.6 shows some of the characteristics that can be sorted into subgroups for better analysis. For example, the employees can be sorted in terms of how many times they download (and presumably read) the company newsletter. Those who download fewer than three times have one thing in common: They are exempt employees (usually management on salary), working in the U.S. and have large supervision loads.

This information can be used in two ways. First, it can help target employees for a campaign. Rather than targeting all employees, a more efficient use of resources would target just those with low newsletter usage. Second, it can pinpoint who to examine in follow-up research. Rather than surveying all employees, a survey or in-depth interviews can focus on low-usage employees. For larger databases, each characteristic (salary employee, location, etc.) can be sorted to refine the target characteristics.

INTERNET TRACKING

Internet tracking is a way to follow the electronic activity of online users. Your Web page "hit" counters provide minimal data, but they can be skewed by "bots," computer programs or search engines that hit Web pages but have no active user. Moreover, a hit does not tell you whether people scrolled down, paid attention or found anything of use.

One way to gather more data is to capture behavior by offering computers a "cookie" that tracks users' Internet behavior. You can determine if users clicked through on any banners you have installed. You will want someone familiar with databases like Microsoft Access to help with this.

Still, this does not provide other variables that you might find helpful, like media use, lifestyle and activities, among others. You likely will need to supplement the database with survey data. There are many commercial services that offer combined tracking with a survey of users.

CULTURAL LIMITATIONS

Different cultures and subcultures respond differently to various techniques. Even within countries, subcultures respond differently to different techniques.

For example, use of the telephone varies from culture to culture. In the United States, it is typical for people to interrupt a conversation to answer a telephone, whereas other cultures consider this rude. Also in the United States, a female is more likely to answer the phone while in other countries a male is more likely to answer. This has implications if you want a gender-balanced sample.

BEING CREATIVE IN SELECTING TECHNIQUES

You are not obligated to select only one technique. Multiple techniques are often used and are preferable when appropriate. In fact, most studies use some mix of techniques.

For example, you may use personal interviews as part of a qualitative study to assess which variables are important and what language to use in your questionnaire, and then you may use the telephone for the survey. Choose the one or two that are appropriate for your needs. Several of the application examples in Chapter 27 use multiple techniques.

CHAPTER 14

QUESTIONNAIRES

Most questionnaires — whether for use over the phone, on the Internet or through the mail — have similar styles, types of questions and wording. Some differences are obvious: A telephone questionnaire must be easily understandable to the ear and Internet questionnaires must fit into the browser frame. This chapter covers the basics of questionnaire design.

IMPORTANCE OF QUESTIONNAIRE DESIGN

Questionnaire design is important because it represents the operationalization of your variables — that is, what you mean by your variables. The questionnaire standardizes how data will be collected, which helps reduce bias and allows for replication.

Before writing a questionnaire, be sure you are familiar with the variables, the data-gathering technique you plan to use and the population for which the technique is intended. Keep in mind that few studies can answer all questions. So you need to set priorities as you begin to trim your questionnaire to a reasonable length.

Although many marketing research firms develop telephone questionnaires that take more than 30 minutes to complete, the ideal length of a general population study should be restricted to about eight minutes for telephone, and a mail survey should be limited to four pages. In-person interviews can be longer, sometimes a half hour or more, and Internet questions have similar restrictions as mail. Longer questionnaires can be used when properly designed and tested. You also need to keep in mind your population because different populations will respond differently to the same question. All questionnaires should be tested by respondents from the target population and an interviewer for usability and "burnout" (getting tired of responding or interviewing).

OPEN-ENDED QUESTIONS

Open-ended questions allow respondents to give any answer they want. These are especially useful when you don't know what the responses are likely to be, such as when you are asking about opinions, attitudes or perceptions that have not been examined by other research.

When you probe for additional thoughts, you can also get more thoughtful or complete answers with open-ends. However, these types of questions should be used with care because they can take a lot of time during an interview and are often difficult to analyze. People with strong opinions might talk on for many minutes if you asked, "What do you think of the job the CEO of your company is doing?" Afterwards, you have to read through various responses and categorize them, which can take a lot of time. Nevertheless, open-ends are important for accessing people's thoughts or words when simpler categories won't suffice or when you want to know if you've missed any possible responses. The following example of an open-end was used by one company because there was no previous research on the topic.

What are the important health care issues to you personally?

_____

_____

(PROBE: Are there any other issues?)

Notice the "probe" which is used to try to elicit a more complete response. Probes are important to make sure that the respondent has had a chance to offer all of his or her thoughts. People tend to limit themselves to the first answer that pops into their head even though they may have several responses. The probe goes beyond the top-of-mind response for more depth or breadth.

Other probes can clarify the meaning of a response, allowing respondents to add their own meaning rather than what the researcher interprets. The following two questions go beyond a simple response like "good." They assess what the person means by "good."

Would you say that your department head does a good, fair or poor job of communicating with you about your work?

(1) GOOD   (2) FAIR   (3) POOR

PROBE: Why do you say (GOOD/FAIR/ POOR)?

_____

_____

(PROBE: Are there any other reasons why you say GOOD/FAIR/POOR?)

The exact words of the respondent are called *verbatims*, from Latin, "in the same words," just as spoken or written by the respondent. The response below shows a verbatim for an open-ended question. Such a response, and several similar to it, proved valuable, causing the hospital to follow up with a subsequent study to explore the need for doctors in the community.

4. What health care issues are important to you personally?

Drs. aren't taking new patients, can't find a Dr.

CLOSED-ENDED QUESTIONS

Closed-ended questions (also called *fixed-response* and *fixed-choice*) require the respondent to select from a list of alternatives. Often this involves asking them to select a number or to answer "yes" or "no." These are especially useful when you know what the responses are likely to be (such as selecting from categories of age) or when you need to force the respondent to select from a list (such as "strongly agree, agree, neutral, disagree, strongly disagree"). These questions are easy to assign numbers to and to analyze.

In the first question shown below the researcher knows most people will answer "yes" or "no." In the second question, the researcher limits the possible responses a maximum of 24 hours.

Do you have access to the Internet?

(1) YES   (2) NO   (3) DON'T KNOW/OTHER RESPONSE

IF YES: On average, how many hours per day do you use the Internet?

_____ (HOURS)

MULTIPLE RESPONSE ITEMS

Many questions either have multiple answers, or you want multiple answers in order to create an *index* (see Chapter 15). In the first question below, respondents can select more than one medium. The second question illustrates multiple responses used for an index to assess how involved respondents are in an upcoming election.

1. What sources would you use if you wanted international news? (CHECK ALL YOU USE)

   ₁☐ Newspaper
   ₁☐ Television
   ₁☐ Magazines
   ₁☐ Radio
   ₁☐ Friends/relatives
   ₁☐ Other: _____

2. Which of the following have you done within the last six months? (CHECK ALL THAT YOU HAVE DONE)

   ₁☐ Voted in the primary election in August?
   ₁☐ Gave money to one of the parties, candidates or issue campaigns?
   ₁☐ Displayed a political sign, button or bumper sticker?
   ₁☐ Attended political meetings or rallies?
   ₁☐ Worked for one of the parties or candidates?
   ₁☐ Tried to influence someone's vote?

"OTHER" RESPONSES

"Other" is a useful response category. The questions in the previous sections are improved with an "other" category that covers responses you may have inadvertently left out. You can then create more categories if you get enough new responses. However, "other" can create problems just like open-ends. If people give many "other" responses, then you will have to take time to code all of those.

CODING

The numbers in the parentheses or next to the boxes in the closed-ended questions above — (3) or ₁□ — represent "codes" for the responses. For example, in a computer data file or spreadsheet, a "1" could represent "yes," "2" is "no" and "3" is "other." Eventually the computer output will show results like: 68 percent for code "1," which means 68 percent "yes." Coding and codebooks will be covered in more detail in Chapter 16.

RULES OF THUMB

Over many decades researchers have acquired a lot of experience creating questions, categories, scales and so on. In addition, they have conducted many experiments to test how well various forms of wording work. These experiments have tested for understanding as well as how to increase response rates and how to obtain more accurate information. These experiences and studies have led to a set of "rules of thumb" for creating good questionnaires.

Regardless of the type of questionnaire you are creating — mail, Internet, phone — you should strive to follow these "rules" because they usually reduce bias and increase efficiency. Reducing bias and making items that are easy and efficient will also lead to collecting more accurate data.

1. FOLLOW YOUR OPERATIONALIZATION

This should be obvious, but it needs to be emphasized. For example, if your operationalization requires you to ask for dollar income because you need "average income," then make sure your questions and responses are in real dollars rather than categories.

2. KEEP EVERYTHING SHORT, SIMPLE AND TO THE POINT

This is efficient and often helps to reduce bias. For example, "How old are you?" is generally a better question than "What was your age at your last birthday?" However, if writing a longer question helps clarify the question for the respondent or reduces bias, then that's OK.

Here's another example: The question — "Now that stock prices have risen, do you plan to invest more money in the next six months?" — may produce a bias because respondents may not have thought about increased stock prices. You should simply ask, "Do you plan to invest more money in the next six months?"

3. WRITE CLEARLY IN THE LANGUAGE OF THE TARGET POPULATION

Avoid using language that respondents cannot understand. Most people working in research and media use jargon that is quite different from that of the general population. We use words like "contemporary hit radio," "publics," "emoticons," "cognitive," and we define "random" and "population" differently than the general public does. Hopefully, you have already done focus groups or other qualitative research with your target population to generate appropriate wording.

4. KEEP A LOGICAL ORDER

Again, this seems obvious. If you want to know how many hours of Internet use people use, ask that question after you have first determined whether they have network access. Logical order also helps prevent bias by keeping questions that might reveal the purpose of your study to the respondent later in the interview. For example, if you need to ask questions about a specific political candidate, you would first pose general questions about the campaign issues so people don't know the name of the candidate(s) upon which you are focusing.

5. PUT SENSITIVE ITEMS AT THE END

For example, asking about money can be offensive and some people do not like to tell their age. When offended, some people refuse to answer any more questions. Saving sensitive questions to the end means that you at least get some usable data.

6. AVOID LEADING OR LOADED QUESTIONS

These are questions that contain an opinion or information that favors one answer or another. Avoiding them can be difficult because you may deal with sensitive issues, but avoid giving information or opinions within a question unless it is absolutely necessary. Even giving what you think is simple information can bias an answer because the respondent may not have had any knowledge to begin with. For example, this question — "The latest poll shows the President with a 67 percent approval rating. Would you rate the President's performance as good, fair or poor?" — risks people giving favorable answers just because they want to be with the majority (the so-called bandwagon effect).

7. AVOID SOCIALLY DESIRABLE RESPONSES

Asking about how much reading a person does will probably be met with exaggeration because people think they're supposed to read more. Similarly, asking about voting leads to estimates of voting that are higher than they actually are. One way to help get more honesty is to guarantee confidentiality and anonymity. Another is to allow people to select a code for a category rather than a word or an open-ended response.

8. AVOID NEGATIVES

"Don't you think the company is doing the best for its employees?" is difficult to answer. It is a "demand" question, begging a "yes" response, but what does "yes" mean — "Yes, I do not" or "Yes, I do?" Orally, people sometimes do not hear the word "not," and visually, while quickly reading a questionnaire, often miss seeing "not."

9. AVOID DOUBLE-BARRELED QUESTIONS

Asking multiple questions at the same time is confusing. For example, "How well run is Company XYZ in your opinion? That is, do you think it is run on a sound business basis?" is two different questions — one about management and one about profitability. Questions that combine topics or ideas can also be confusing, such as, "Do you think Starbucks is good for the community and a good employer?" Is "yes" a response to both or only one part?

10. BE PRECISE

Imprecise terms and phrases can be confusing or difficult. For example, the question — "Do you listen to the radio regularly?" — is problematic. What does "regularly" mean? Daily? Five hours per day? "Did you listen yesterday?" is better, but "How many hours of radio did you listen to yesterday?" is the most precise.

11. MANY ITEMS REQUIRE A TIME FRAME

This is similar to being precise. See the time frame in italics in the following examples. Do not ask, "How much money do you plan to spend on suits and other dress attire?" Instead ask, "How much money do you plan to spend on suits and other dress attire *within the next six months*?" Do not ask, "What is your income?" Instead ask, "What is you *annual* household income?" When asking about behavior you often need to consider using "yesterday," "in an average week," "during the next year," and other time parameters.

12. DON'T WRITE BY COMMITTEE

Many styles of writing are acceptable as long as they conform to the language of the target population. However, committees get bogged down in the minutia of questions and responses, each member trying to impose her or his style on the questions. This wastes time. However, it is important to have others review your work, so you can have committees make sure the questions match the operationalizations and your original needs and goals.

13. ALWAYS ASK, "CAN THE RESPONDENT ANSWER THE QUESTIONS?"

Imagine if you were asked to provide the salaries of the employees you supervise. You might have to look that information up. If you were asked if you were using your wireless phone or listening to music last June 28, you probably couldn't answer because you couldn't remember.

14. LAYOUT IS IMPORTANT

Telephone questionnaires should be easy to read and fill out by the interviewer. Mail questionnaires should be easy to read and fill out by the recipient. Internet questionnaires should be easy to read and scroll or page through, and the type needs to be big enough to read easily.

15. RULES CAN BE BROKEN IF THERE IS A GOOD REASON

I once put a sensitive question about race first in a telephone questionnaire. The reason was that the target was African-American radio listeners, and there were only 8 percent African-Americans in the market. If the question had been last, then the study would have required a sample of almost 4,000 people to get about 300 interviews within my target population. Saving many thousands of dollars was worth the risk of upsetting a few respondents.

LAYOUT

Layout is obviously important to the respondent when filling out a mail or online questionnaire, but it is also important for interviewers who need to see questions clearly and find responses quickly. Some common guidelines for questionnaires that respondents fill out include:

- Provide enough "white space" or space between and around the questions and responses so they are easy to find.
- Use common type faces and sizes (*script* fonts are especially difficult to read).
- Provide clear instructions, both at the beginning and within the questionnaire.
- Provide enough space for written responses.

Some common guides to help interviewers include:

- Provide enough "white space" or space between and around the questions and responses so they are easy to find and read.
- Make clear what should be asked or shown and what should not, such as using ALL CAPS to indicate directions or categories and lower-case to indicate the questions and responses that should be read to the respondent.
- Provide enough space for verbatims and comments.

PRE-TEST, PRE-TEST, PRE-TEST

There are unforseen ways that a questionnaire can fail. For example, once I used a question about Internet pornography in a telephone questionnaire, but when "real" people were interviewed they laughed or tittered . So I dropped the scale item.

How do you know if you have been successful in following the rules of thumb? How do you know if you have written in a language people can read or your Internet questionnaire is usable in Internet Explorer and Netscape? *Pre-test, pre-test, pre-test.*

Before you use your questionnaire *pre-test* it! That is, let some "real" people try to fill out the questionnaire on a computer or in person or respond on the phone. You can use a small sample study for this. Debrief these people, asking what they didn't understand, found confusing or unclear, or found difficult to answer. Rewrite the questionnaire and pre-test it again. Do this long enough before you plan to start data collection so you can make necessary changes.

CHAPTER 15

INDEXES AND SCALES

Some variables cannot be accurately measured with a single question or a single set of categories. Imagine trying to understand the image people have of your company by just asking one question: "Is your image of XYZ Company positive or negative?" All this would elicit is the percentage of the population that is positive or negative. You would not know two important things: the *magnitude* of their position, or how strongly they felt; and what they *meant* by their position, or what is the meaning of "positive" or "negative."

Consequently, we use multiple-item indexes and scales to give us more precise measures of these variables. An *index* or *scale* is simply a series of items or statements with varying response categories that are totaled to get a scale score. The *scale score* is a measure of the amount of the characteristic (attitude, image, knowledge, etc.) and usually is assumed to represent an interval level of measurement.

INDEXES

Indexes are the simplest type of multiple-item measures and are usually used to assess magnitude of knowledge or behavior, such as how many things a person owns and how often a person participates in an activity. Indexes are similar to checklists except that indexes are mathematically summed, giving "how many" or "how much" of a variable a person has.

For example, predicting whether someone will purchase newly developed technology or software is partly dependent on the number of technologies they currently own. That number can be generated by asking people to check off what they have. To get the total just add up the "checks" and people can be targeted by the number of technologies they own.

Do you own any of the following? (CHECK ALL THAT YOU OWN)

- ☐ Personal computer
- ☐ Satellite dish
- ☐ VCR
- ☐ DVD player
- ☐ Cell phone
- ☐ High definition or digital TV
- ☐ Digital still camera
- ☐ Digital or CCD video camera
- ☐ iPod or other portable digital music system
- ☐ Others (please list them): _____

_____

TOTAL CHECKED: _____

Probably the most used index in universities is the infamous "multiple-guess" exam, usually composed of a set of items with the total number of correct choices being the scale score or test score. The level of measurement in these examples is "ratio" — real numbers from zero to the maximum possible correct items.

Another example comes from political campaigns. The same question was used to illustrate multiple responses in the previous chapter. Now we use it as an index because the total score is used to assess level of political participation. Assessments of political participation help differentiate people who are heavily involved in campaigns from others. These indexes involve more than just whether people vote. Once again you would add up the number of activities checked to get a total political participation score.

Which of the following have you done within the last six months? (CHECK ALL THAT YOU HAVE DONE)

- ☐ Voted in the primary election in August.
- ☐ Gave money to one of the parties, candidates or issue campaigns.
- ☐ Displayed a political sign, button or bumper sticker.
- ☐ Attended political meetings or rallies.

☐ Worked for one of the parties or candidates.
☐ Tried to influence someone's vote.

TOTAL CHECKED: _____

SCALES

Scales consist of multiple items or questions used to measure a single variable. They posses the following characteristics:

- Usually composed of four or more items or questions
- Have a large selection of responses — e.g., "strongly agree, agree, neutral, disagree, strongly disagree" or "On a scale of 0 to 100 percent"
- Are summed to obtain a numeric "scale score"
- Are assumed to be at least interval level of measurement

The most popular scale for opinions and attitudes is the *Likert scale*, which contains a set of response categories from "strongly agree" to "strongly disagree."

Circle whether you strongly agree, agree, are neutral or don't know, disagree or strongly disagree with each item below.

1. XYZ company plays a part in my community. (CIRCLE ONE)

Strongly Agree   Agree   Neutral/Don't know   Disagree   Strongly Disagree

2. XYZ company is not trustworthy. (CIRCLE ONE)

Strongly Agree   Agree   Neutral/Don't know   Disagree   Strongly Disagree

Other scales are similar. They have a set of statements but differ in style or number of response categories. Response categories can change, such as using "very satisfied" to "very dissatisfied."

How satisfied are you with the following when you shop for clothing at ABC Department Store? (CIRCLE ONE FOR EACH ITEM)

	Very Satisfied	Somewhat Satisfied	Neutral	Somewhat Dissatisfied	Very Dissatisfied
1. Variety of styles	5	4	3	2	1
2. Prices	5	4	3	2	1
3. Helpfulness of salespeople	5	4	3	2	1

The response categories can take on a variety of meanings depending on what you are trying to measure. You can assess interest, familiarity, support, how often people do behaviors, how well something is perceived, and many other things. You can use a number of different evaluative scales:

- Very Interested, Somewhat Interested, Neutral, Somewhat Uninterested, Very Uninterested
- Very Familiar, Somewhat Familiar, Neutral, Somewhat Unfamiliar, Very Unfamiliar
- Strongly Support, Support, Neutral, Against, Strongly Against
- Almost Always, Usually, Sometimes, Not Very Often, Never
- Excellent, Good, Fair, Poor

The *Semantic Differential scale* uses "polar adjectives" as items to represent the extremes of positions people can take toward a concept. These can be "hot/cold," "never/always," "good/bad," etc. Between the adjectives is an odd number of responses, often spaces or boxes, that the respondent selects to show how close they are to that adjective. For example, in the scale below if you think XYZ Company (the concept) is as modern (the polar adjective) as possible you would check the box closest to modern.

XYZ Company

| Modern | ⊠ | ☐ | ☐ | ☐ | ☐ | ☐ | ☐ | Old-Fashioned |
| | 7 | 6 | 5 | 4 | 3 | 2 | 1 | |

| Progressive | ⊠ | ☐ | ☐ | ☐ | ☐ | ☐ | ☐ | Backward |
| | 7 | 6 | 5 | 4 | 3 | 2 | 1 | |

| Bad | ☐ | ☐ | ☐ | ☐ | ☐ | ☐ | ⊠ | Good |
| | 1 | 2 | 3 | 4 | 5 | 6 | 7 | |

Notice that the adjectives "modern," "progressive" and "good" have a positive connotation and "old," "intransigent" and "bad" have a negative connotation. Do not put all "positive" adjectives on the same side in order to avoid *response bias*, which occurs when some people just select the same response all the way down the list without giving much thought to the answer. Alternating the "positive" and "negative" items forces them to be more considerate in their answer.

Notice also that the scoring is different when the "positive" adjective is on the right versus the left. To be consistent you have to have higher numbers next to positive adjectives so that higher totals represent more positive attitudes. In the example above, the X-ed answers are 7 + 7 + 7 for a total of 21, the most positive score. If someone checked "7" and "6" and "4" their score would be 17, still positive but not as strong as the first score.

You're probably wondering, "How long should a scale be?" They should be long enough to be reliable but short enough so they are not wasting time. That involves analyzing the scale for reliability and dropping items that do not contribute to reliability. In practice, the limit is about four to 20 items.

PRECISION SCALING

In Chapter 7 you learned that being precise allows you to be more accurate. Sometimes you want to be more precise than just the five or seven responses in the Likert or Semantic Differential scales. Consider that two people may say "strongly agree," yet one person feels "*very* strongly" and the other is just simply "strongly," and you want to be able to distinguish between those people. You may also use a different style of response because it is more appropriate for the scale or item you are using, like using percentages to estimate how often a person can trust what your company says — "0 percent of the time to 100 percent of the time."

To obtain more precise measures of strength in scales, use *direct magnitude estimates*, which means using integers to measure magnitude or size with a range of numbers, usually "0 to 10," "1 to 10" or "0 percent to 100 percent." The following example assesses the magnitude of importance of various characteristics with "1 to 10." You could try to assess the importance of characteristics in managers by using statements like "Friendliness in a boss is important to me" and have the responses be "strongly agree to strongly disagree," but notice that there are twice as many choices with direct magnitude estimates — 10 in the example below vs. five for "SA to SD."

Please circle the number for each attribute that represents how important that characteristic is when you talk with your boss.

Least Important <----------------> Most Important

Friendliness	1	2	3	4	5	6	7	8	9	10
Treats me with respect	1	2	3	4	5	6	7	8	9	10
Allows me to talk	1	2	3	4	5	6	7	8	9	10
Meets at the appointed time	1	2	3	4	5	6	7	8	9	10

Direct magnitude estimates can be used either for single items or scales. For example, if you want employees to rate the quality of communication between themselves and management, instead of using "good, fair, poor" as responses, you could use "zero to 100, where zero means the lowest quality and 100 means the highest quality."

> On a scale of zero to 100, with zero meaning not effective at all and 100 meaning very effective, how would you rate the following between you and your supervisor?
>
> _____ Informing you about changes in company policies
> _____ Listening to your concerns about the job
> _____ Letting you know how well you are doing

Other less-used scales include *Guttman* and *Thurstone*. *Guttman* scales are assumed to be in a continuum such that each item depends on the answer to the previous item. For example, if someone said that they liked to shop for many different specific products you would expect that they would also like to shop in general.

Thurstone scales create equal-appearing intervals by using a very large number of statements that are rated by a large sample of people. Scale score values are computed for each item. This helps solve the problem that intervals between responses (e.g., between "agree," "neutral" and "disagree") aren't equal.

WHERE DO INDEXES AND SCALES COME FROM?

If you were to think of items to measure the image of your company, you might miss some that people from other social classes or academic and professional backgrounds consider important. There is an eight-step process to follow that will help you generate a scale in the language and based on the importance of concepts to your target population.

> Step 1. *Collect concepts and statements* that describe the different aspects of your variable. For example, a company's image depends on many factors: how people rate its ability to do its job, how well it fits into the community, how it treats its employees and how well it communicates with the public. How do you know what those are? Ask people. Conduct in-depth interviews or focus groups or use some other qualitative research where people can talk both generally and specifically about your company.

Step 2. *Write a set of statements* based on those concepts and statements. Use the words of your target as much as possible. For example, if the comments are: "I'm really concerned that the hospital has the latest technology" and "They need to be concerned about our community," items might be:

1. Regional Hospital has the latest technology.
2. Regional Hospital cares about the tri-county community.
3. They use the latest technology.

Step 3. *Eliminate redundant expressions.* There are several different ways people can talk about the latest technology: "Has the latest technology," "Is up on technology," or "Use the latest technology." Pick the simplest expression.

Step 4. *Some items should be negative and some positive.* This is to avoid response bias. If the initial interviews have not already generated enough negative items, the easy way to do this is to randomly change half of the items to negative statements (for random assignment see Chapter 19).

1. Regional Hospital has the latest technology.
2. Regional Hospital does not care about the tri-county community.

Step 5. *Randomly order the statements or items.* This avoids unconscious bias on your part. Some researchers also randomly order the statements for each interview using Computer Assisted Telephone Interviewing (CATI) software.

Step 6. *Determine the style of the scale.* Will it be Likert or Semantic Differential or something else? Assign numbers to each response (reversed for negative statements). Notice that the numbering is reversed for the second or negative item; SD is actually a positive response and gets a "5."

1. Regional Hospital has the latest technology.

SA	A	N	D	SD
5	4	3	2	1

2. Regional Hospital cares little about the tri-county community.

SA	A	N	D	SD
1	2	3	4	5

Step 7. *Test the scale before using it.* Pre-testing can be done with a small group of about 20 to 100 people. You can use a convenience sample, but make sure you have a variety of types of people with different demographics, geography, etc. If you're using the scale over the phone, test it on the phone; if it's by mail, have people fill it out by hand. After they fill out the scale, debrief them, asking if there were any items they couldn't understand, anything that was confusing, and any other possible problems they had.

If the group was large enough (50 or more), you can do some statistical analyses to examine whether the items go together and whether there are redundancies. Correlation will tell whether two items are redundant (high positive or negative) and factor analysis and reliability will tell whether the items relate to each other enough to form a scale (see *multivariate analysis* in Chapter 25). Eliminate redundant and unrelated items, and there it is — the tentative final scale. I say "tentative" because the scale must be used in a real study to make a final determination of its usefulness.

Step 8. *Test it again.*

A SCALE EXAMPLE

To illustrate the usefulness of a scale, let's look at a scale that defines roles (or jobs) in public relations companies. Job titles are often insufficient or inaccurate to do this. That's because a vice president's responsibilities at one company may differ greatly from a vice president's at another, or an account executive for one firm may play the same role as a sales associate at another.

Among public relations professionals, there is a difference between people who perform primarily a technical role, such as producing press releases, vs. those who perform a managerial role, such as communicating with management and the public. In response to this, academics and professionals have developed and refined what is called the "Public Relations Practitioner Roles Scale."

This scale was originally developed by Glen Broom and George Smith in 1979 and refined into a two-role scale by Glen Broom and David Dozier in 1986. Here is an abridged version of that scale just to demonstrate scale use. The eight items come from 24 original items. It is a two-part scale, obtaining two scores, one for the manager role (first four items) and one for the technician role (next four items).

Communication Manager Role:

1. I make the information policy decisions.

   SA A N D SD
   ⑤   4 3 2   1

2. I do not keep management informed of public reactions to organizational policies, procedures and/or actions.

   SA A N D SD
   1   2 3 ④ 5

3. In meetings with management, I point out the need to follow a systematic public relations planning process.

   SA A N D SD
   ⑤   4 3 2   1

4. I do not plan and recommend courses of action for solving public relations problems.

   SA A N D SD
   1   2 3 ④ 5

Technician Role:

5. I am not the person who writes information material.

   SA A N D SD
   1   ② 3 4   5

6. I produce brochures, pamphlets and other publications.

   SA A N D SD
   5   4 3 ②   1

7. I maintain media contacts.

   SA A N D SD
   5   ④ 3 2   1

8. I do not place news releases.

   SA A N D SD
   1   ② 3 4   5

The above items form two scales, measuring either the management or the technical function. Note that a respondent can score high on both or on only one. The responses above get the following scores: 18 for "Communication Manager" and 10 for "Technician." So this person plays more of a managerial roll but some technician role. In a real study you would randomly mix the items, and the roles of communication manager and technician would not be mentioned so we wouldn't bias the respondent.

CHAPTER 16

CODING DATA AND CODEBOOKS

Y ou have already read about codes in an earlier chapter. This involves assigning numbered responses for questions or numbering the categories on a scale. Coding is important because it connects the observations you make with your analysis.

CODING

Coding is simply turning responses into usable entries for a data or computer file. You try to create codes as much as possible before you conduct a study.

In the following example, notice the numbers next to the responses in the fixed-response questions. You might assign "1" as the code for "yes" and "2" as the code for "no" for question one. The "-" indicates that the response is coded "blank" — no entry is made. In question two, "1" means "good," "2" means "fair" and "3" means "poor." Those are the numbers that you enter into your spreadsheet or that would be entered automatically in a CATI system or Web-page database.

1.   Do you have access to the Internet?

   (1) YES   (2) NO   (-) DON'T KNOW/OTHER

2. Would you say your department head does a good, fair or poor job of communicating with you about your job?

(1) GOOD   (2) FAIR   (3) POOR

Check-off lists are a little different. In the following example, you just want to know whether or not a person checked the item. In essence each item is a separate variable. That is, did they say "yes" to "newspaper," "yes" to "television" and so on? So you might assign "1" if they checked the item and "0" to indicate they did not check it.

What sources would you use if you wanted international news?
(CHECK ALL THAT YOU USE)

₁☐ NEWSPAPER
₁☐ TELEVISION
₁☐ MAGAZINES
₁☐ RADIO
₁☐ INTERNET
₁☐ OTHER: _____

Indexes and scales are different than check-off lists. You need to decide how you will code each response plus whether you will calculate the scale score with your statistical software or whether you will first calculate the scale score by hand and enter only the score in the spreadsheet. For the political participation scale below, you could enter a "1" for each item if checked and a "0" if not, or you might go through each questionnaire, compute the total and enter that total into your spreadsheet. In this case, two items are checked and a "2" is entered.

Did you do any of the following within the last six months?
(CHECK ALL THAT APPLY)

₁☐ Voted in the primary election in August
₁☒ Gave money to one of the parties, candidates or issue campaigns
₁☒ Displayed a political sign, button or bumper sticker
₁☐ Attended political meetings or rallies
₁☐ Worked for one of the parties or candidates
₁☐ Tried to influence someone's vote

TOTAL CHECKED ___2___

The next example may come from a mail questionnaire. You could enter each item separately, that is a "7" is entered for "modern/old fashioned," a "7" for "progressive/intransigent" and a "7" for "bad/good." Then those three variables are added together to form a new variable for the total scale score.

XYZ Company

Modern	☒ ☐ ☐ ☐ ☐ ☐ ☐ 7 6 5 4 3 2 1	Old fashioned
Progressive	☒ ☐ ☐ ☐ ☐ ☐ ☐ 7 6 5 4 3 2 1	Intransigent
Bad	☐ ☐ ☐ ☐ ☐ ☐ ☒ 1 2 3 4 5 6 7	Good

SCALE SCORE ___21___

CODING OPEN-ENDS/VERBATIMS

Open-ends and verbatims from probes in surveys, in-depth interviews and transcripts from focus groups are usually not as easily coded as the above examples.

You may choose just to list the responses and summarize by counting how many of each response there are (see Table16.1, where responses to "What is your one general impression of Kadlec Medical Center?" are simply listed). You could also create categories and codes for the Kadlec responses. For example, you could code "positive" responses "1" and "negative" responses "2."

There can be problems coding the meaning of ambiguous comments like "a corporation." For those comments you should conduct a coding session with multiple coders and try to arrive at a consensus for interpreting the comments.

CODEBOOKS

Codebooks contain a list of variables along with how those variables were operationalized and the coding of the responses. When the study is complete a copy of the codebook and data file are kept along with the report so you can correctly interpret the report or do additional analyses later. With a copy of the codebook and a copy of the computer data file, you can conduct your own analysis of the data and write a report based on how the data were acquired (what questions or what scales

Table 16.1
LIST OF OPEN-ENDED COMMENTS
(Used by permission of Kadlec Medical Center)

Good (22 mentions)	Suck
Pretty good (14)	Advanced technology
Professional (9)	A corporation
Fine (9)	Bright and cheery
OK/fair (6)	E.R. pitiful
Excellent (6)	Long wait at ER
Favorable (5)	Busy place
Modern (5)	Billing blood suckers
Like it (5)	Snobbish
Too slow (5)	Helpful
Efficient (4)	Competent
Clean (4)	Overpriced
Improved (2)	As reputable as others
Better than others (2)	Rapacious
Cold people	

were used). Codebooks can be informal or formal. An informal codebook might just be a copy of the questionnaire. A formal codebook might use the style in Table 16.2. It describes a companion spreadsheet wherein Column A contains the ID number, Column B contains codes for the Internet access variable, etc.

This codebook shows how to enter data in a spreadsheet or how to interpret data from a spreadsheet or statistical software. Each interview would be a row in the spreadsheet and each column would represent a variable. For example, Column A in the spreadsheet is the ID number, Column B is the "Internet access" variable and it would have a "1," "2" or "3," etc. In Table 16.3, Column A shows the interview ID for the row, Column B shows Internet access (ID's 1, 2 and 4 have access; ID 3 does not), etc.

JOEY REAGAN

Table16.2
EXAMPLE CODEBOOK

COL	Variable	Question/Item	Meaning of Codes
A	ID		Unique INTERVIEW ID; 001 thru 325
B	Internet access	Do you have access to the Internet?	1=yes; 2=no BLANK=don't know/ other respns
C	Department head evaluation	Would you say your department head does a good, fair or poor job of communicating with you about your job?	1=good; 2=fair 3=poor
D	International news source: newspapers	What sources would you use if you wanted international news?	1=checked yes 0=did not check
E	International news source: television	What sources would you use if you wanted international news?	1=checked yes 0=did not check
F	International news source: magazines	What sources would you use if you wanted international news?	1=checked yes 0=did not check
G	International news source: radio	What sources would you use if you wanted international news?	1=checked yes 0=did not check
H	International news source: Internet	What sources would you use if you wanted international news?	1=checked yes 0=did not check
I	International news source: other	What sources would you use if you wanted international news?	1=checked yes 0=did not check
J	Political Participation Scale	Did you do any of the following within the last six months? – Voted in the primary election in August – Gave money to one of the parties, candidates or issue campaigns – Displayed a political sign, button or bumper sticker – Attended political meetings or rallies	NUMBER=total number checked
K	Semantic Differential Scale: XYZ Company (Item 1)	Polar adjectives: Modern/Old	7, 6, 5, 4, 3, 2, 1
L	Semantic Differential Scale: XYZ Company (Item 2)	Polar adjectives: Progressive/Intransigent	7, 6, 5, 4, 3, 2, 1
M	Semantic Differential Scale: XYZ Company (Item 3)	Polar adjectives: Bad/Good	1, 2, 3, 4, 5, 6, 7

With so much data being collected, stored and analyzed electronically many codebooks are only available electronically. Figure 16.1 shows the codebook for the "General Social Survey," conducted by the National Opinion Research Center at the

Table16.3
EXAMPLE SPREADSHEET BASED ON THE CODEBOOK

A	B	C	D	E	F	G	H	I	J	K	L	M
1	1	2	1	1	1	1	1	1	1	6	4	6
2	1	3	1	1	0	1	1	0	6	5	6	6
3	2	1	1	1	0	0	0	0	2	7	6	3
4	1	1	1	1	0	0	0	0	0	2	2	3

University of Chicago and posted at the University of Michigan Survey Research Center Web site. The codebook contains links to all essential information, each variable's description and descriptions of how the study was conducted (links to the questionnaire, reports, etc.).

Figure 16.1
ONLINE CODEBOOK
(Used by permission of NORC, University of Chicago)

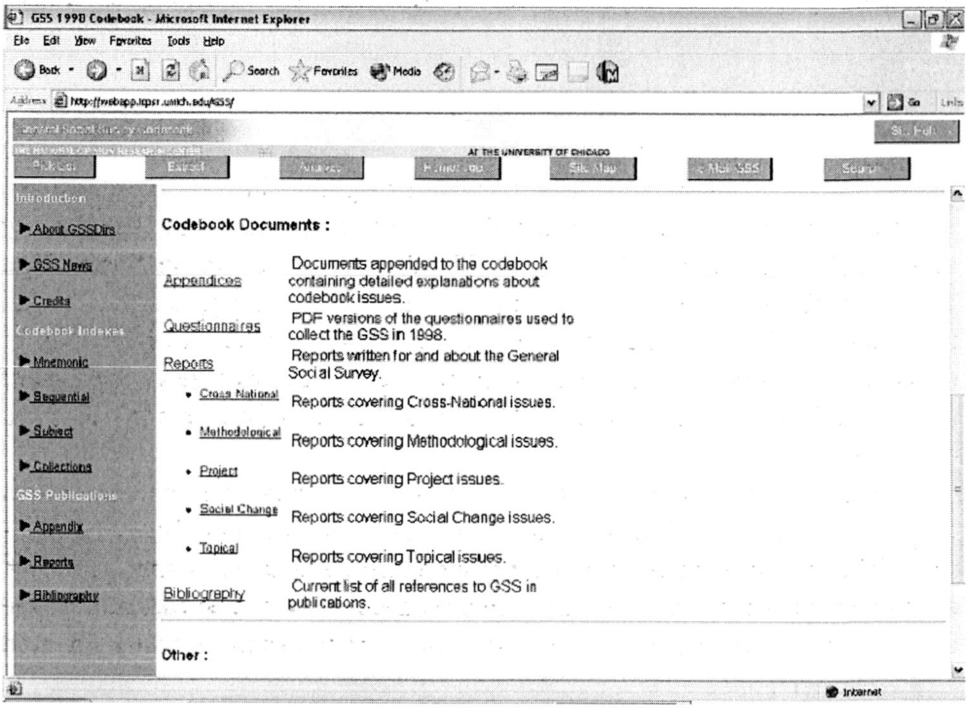

JOEY REAGAN

CHAPTER 17

THE NORMAL CURVE

T his chapter is rather abstract, but that is the nature of studying the *normal curve*. The curve provides the theoretical foundation for sampling and analysis in social science research. Like some other concepts in the social sciences, understanding this will help you understand the basis for confidence in the methods we use.

WHAT IS THE NORMAL CURVE?

The *normal curve* represents the distribution of probabilities of equally likely events. For example, if you flip a coin, the normal curve represents the probability of getting HTHTHT, or HHHHHH, or TTTTT, or any other combination of flips. The most likely events to occur are mixtures of heads and tails. They are represented by large areas under the curve, represented by the peak in the middle of the curve in Figure17.1. Other less likely events, such as a very long runs of heads or tails, are represented by small areas called the "tails" on the left and right of the curve.

   This same analysis applies to random samples in social science. The normal curve represents all possible samples that can be drawn from a population. Chapters 18 and 19 will cover more detail about randomness and how to sample. Random sampling assumes each element has an equal chance of being selected, similar to the equal chance of getting a head or a tail. Most of the samples will be a good

Figure 17.1
THE NORMAL CURVE

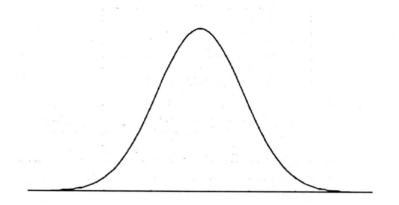

representation of the population, getting about equal males and females, proportional distributions for education and income that are close to that of the population, and so on. Those samples are located in the middle of the curve. Very few will be "skewed" and won't be very good representations of the population, having mostly females or mostly high-income people. Those samples are located in the "tails"of the curve.

The normal curve also represents the probabilities that a sample statistic is an accurate representation of the population, and many significance tests use the normal curve. Given all of the uses for the normal curve, it is not surprising that researchers spend a lot of time studying it, and that you need to understand it.

AREAS UNDER THE CURVE

In order to use the normal curve to calculate probabilities about samples and to make inferences from samples, you need to know some basic terminology associated with it.

The total area under the curve is 1.0 or 100 percent. How much of the curve's area you use to estimate a probability depends on how far out from the center toward the tails you go. This depends on the *standard deviation*: how many "standard units" you deviate from the center. (Standard deviation is usually abbreviated "sd.") You go out from the center (0.0sd), to +1.0sd to the right or −1.0sd to the left or some other standard units.

JOEY REAGAN

Figure 17.2
STANDARD DEVIATION FROM THE MEAN

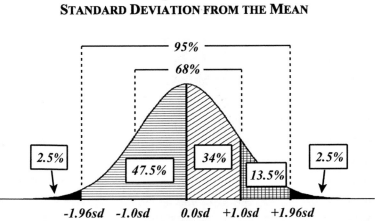

In Figure 17.2, if you go out to the right +1.0sd, the area between 0.0sd and 1.0sd is 34 percent of the area under the curve. It is the same if you go to the left −1.0sd. If you go both ways, ±1.0sd, the area is twice as much or 68 percent of the area. That means the probability is 68 percent that random events between ±1.0sd will occur.

Social scientists use a specific standard deviation for most of their calculations: ±1.96sd. This standard deviation is the basis or rule of thumb for calculating sampling error (see Chapter 20) and acceptable probabilities for doing significance tests (see Chapter 24). In Figure 17.2 notice that going out −1.96sd contains 47.5 percent of the curve. Going out both directions or ±1.96sd contains 95 percent of the area under the curve. What's left in each tail is 2.5 percent or 5 percent for both. These two figures — 95 percent and 5 percent — are important. They represent the probability that we are accurate with our research estimates (95%), and conversely, the probability of being inaccurate (5%).

CONFIDENCE LEVEL AND CONFIDENCE INTERVAL

Two other concepts relate to the normal curve. The first is *confidence level*, which is a probability. If you go out ±1.0sd, then the probability or confidence level is 68 percent. If you go out ±1.96sd then the probability or confidence level is 95 percent.

Confidence interval is a range of numbers that relates to the confidence level. If the confidence level is 68 percent, then the range or confidence interval

Figure 17.3
RANGE OF VALUES, ±1.96SD, FOR A 64 PERCENT RESULT

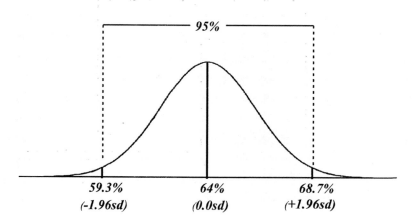

corresponds to ±1.0sd. If the confidence level is 95 percent, the confidence interval corresponds to ±1.96sd.

The examples in the next section will illustrate this with a confidence level of 95 percent and a confidence interval of ±1.96sd. These terms will come up again in Chapter 20 when you calculate sampling error.

APPLYING THE CURVE TO RESEARCH RESULTS

In each of the two examples that follow, I have assumed a sample size of 400; thus, you will be able to replicate these calculations when you have read Chapter 20 about sampling error.

For the first example (see Figure 17.3), let's say you have used a random sample to conduct a survey of consumers, and the results show that 64 percent plan to purchase an automobile within the next six months. The normal curve says there is a 95 percent probability that the "true population value" falls within the confidence interval or range of 64 percent ±1.96sd. The standard deviation shows that ±1.96sd is ±4.7 percent. That means we are confident the population percentage is close to the sample percentage and that we are 95 percent sure that it lies within ±4.7 percent — between 59.3 percent and 68.7 percent. In Figure 17.3 you can see the estimate in the middle and the range of percentages for ±1.96sd.

For the second example (see Figure 17.4), suppose you are using ratings to

Figure 17.4
RANGE OF VALUES, ±1.96SD, FOR AN 11 RATING

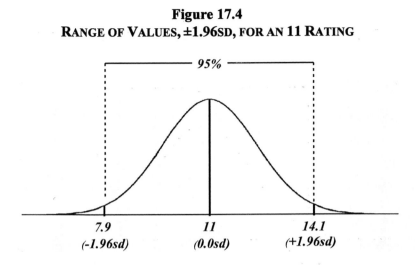

7.9	11	14.1
(-1.96sd)	*(0.0sd)*	*(+1.96sd)*

estimate TV audiences. Ratings are based on random samples, and the number itself is a percentage estimate — a rating of 11 means 11 percent of the audience. The calculation shows a range of ±3.1 rating points. The estimate is "11," but there is a 95 percent probability that the "true population values" is between 7.9 and 14.1.

These two examples should seem familiar because they are similar to polls and surveys you have seen in the media. Usually, the story of the poll will say something like, "This study is subject to an error of 4 percent." What they are really saying is that there is a 95 percent probability that the real population numbers fall within the range of ±4.0 percent.

OTHER PROBABILITY DISTRIBUTIONS

The normal curve is not the only probability distribution that researchers use. Others are used for statistical tests: "chi-square," "*F*," "*t*," "*u*,"and others, some of which are covered in Chapter 24.

CHAPTER 18

WHY USE A SAMPLE

At this point it is time to decide whether to use a sample. Keep in mind that concepts like *random* and *population* and *sample* mean something quite different to researchers than they do to most other people. So before looking at samples, you need to become familiar with concepts related to sampling.

POPULATIONS AND SAMPLES

A *population* is the collection of individuals or objects about which you want information. It must be precisely defined. Do you mean people or things? Remember, you can study a competitor's ads as well as a target population. Do you mean all of a group or just a subset? You can study all people in San Diego or just men, 18-35, in San Diego. Do you mean individuals or households or families?

Often populations are referred to as "target public," "target population," "target market," or simply "target." A population is also a "constant" (remember the difference between constant and variable in Chapter 5?). Examples of populations include:

- U.S. registered voters
- U.S. men
- Residents of Sacramento, California
- Households in Dade County, Florida
- My competitors' TV advertisements for the last four weeks

- All news stories about my company in the local newspaper and local broadcast news in the last 12 months
- My company's employees

A *sample* is a subset of the population which is used to gather information about the population as a whole. It should "reflect" the population accurately. The goal is to make an inference from the sample to the population. In order to make that inference, we need to *randomly* sample the population. Ordinarily, researchers mean a random sample when referring to samples. Sometimes you may use a non-random sample, but you can't use it to make inferences to a population.

SHOULD I DO CENSUS OR SURVEY?

A *census* is an attempt to gather information about *all* members of a population. A census is not a sample. If you gather information from everyone, you have not used a sample.

If the population is small, it might make sense to gather information from everyone rather than use a sample. If you had a company with 150 employees, it would be easy to gather data from all employees. If you wanted to examine all local newspaper print ads for your competitors in the last month and you had one local metro daily paper, then you could easily look through all 30 issues and cut out all stories about your company. Just remember that you are doing a census, not a survey. This is an important distinction when you get to sampling error and significance tests. With a census you do not have sampling error.

However, if the population is large — 50,000 residents, all television ads in the last year or 12,000 employees — then it is more time- and cost-efficient to use a sample. In addition, you should consider samples for small populations under special circumstances. When conducting multiple studies on the same population, such as longitudinal research, you do not want to sensitize everyone to the research. You might randomly split employees into two groups because you don't want to expose all employees to the issues you are asking about, which would sensitize them to pay more attention than they otherwise would, or you may not wish to burden people with too many tasks making them less likely to participate in later surveys, or you may not want people getting tired of participating in a study which would make their responses less reliable (known as "research burnout").

Still, the most important reason for using a sample is that you have a large population and want an economical study with accurate inferences to the population.

WHAT IS A SAMPLE?

As noted above, a sample is a subset of a population that is used to make an inference to that population. Making an *inference* means that you take an observation from the sample and project it onto the population — confident that your results are close to what you would find in the population if you did a census. Note the word "close."

For example, if you found that 65 percent of your sample planned to buy deli meat products in the next month, you would infer that around 65 percent (not exactly 65 percent) of the population planned to buy deli meat products in the next month. The "65 percent" is an estimate, not an exact number. But in order to faithfully mirror the population, you need to be confident that the sample is *representative* of the population. That confidence comes from *random* sampling, covered in a later section in this chapter and using the techniques in Chapter 19.

Richard Harket, vice president of Coleman Research, writing in the National Association of Broadcaster's book *Radio in Search of Excellence,* expressed the essential characteristics of populations and samples: "Research enables a radio station to speak to a few hundred listeners with the confidence that the opinions of these reflect the opinions of all listeners in equal proportions." He refers to "a few hundred listeners" (the sample) reflecting the opinions of "all listeners" (the population). Thus, a sample is not an exact correspondence to the population but a "reflection" of the population.

Some people use the terms *probability sample* and *nonprobability sample* to refer to random samples and nonrandom samples, respectively. This makes sense because when we calculate sampling error, it is based on probability, and when we do statistical tests, the result is a probability and these calculations assume random samples. It is only with random samples that we can know the probability related to our data. Thus, "probability" and "random" go together.

WHAT IS RANDOM?

Random has a specific meaning to researchers that is different than what people normally mean by the term. Random does *not* mean arbitrary, incidental, odd or confused. Random is *the equal chance for all events in a pool of events to happen.* Applied to sampling, random means the equal chance for all members of a population to be in the sample.

For instance, when applied to telephone numbers, it is the equal chance for each telephone number to be in the sample. Applied to names on a list, it is the equal chance for each name to be part of the sample.

Most people think of random as arbitrary, like "put your finger in the middle of the phone book," or "pick a number from one to ten," or "randomly stop someone on the street," or "pick a card at random from the deck." These and similar methods are *not* random. They are what statisticians call *systematically biased*. As humans we have systems. We tend to favor one selection over another. For example, people tend to pick the middle of the phone book (giving those numbers a better chance of being selected), and they avoid extremes in a list of one to ten (numbers 4, 5, and 6 have a better chance of being selected). Try it on your friends.

We can use the concept of random in many ways. Selecting samples like random telephone numbers is an obvious one, but we can also use it to make selections when we want to reduce our biases, such as how to order questions in a scale, or how to assign tasks to employees when there are ten people who are equally qualified.

GENERALIZABILITY OF SAMPLES

Generalizability is the ability to apply results from your study to its population or the applicability of the sample to the population. Keep in mind that any data you collect from a random sample are generalizable *only* to the population from which you drew the sample. Different populations, even from the same city or state, have different subcultures, habits, tastes, opinions, behaviors, values and so on.

So if you draw a sample of adults, it doesn't represent teenagers. If you draw a sample in Boston, it doesn't represent Los Angeles or Massachusetts. If you draw a sample of skiers, it doesn't represent all active people. Generalizability is tied to representativeness. If the sample matches the population, then it is representative, and you can generalize to that population (see Chapter 23 for more about how to tell whether a sample is representative).

CAN I USE NONRANDOM SAMPLES?

The answer is "no" if you want to make inferences to populations. The answer is "yes" if you understand the limitations of nonrandom samples. You can use them for many qualitative studies or to do pre-testing. Nonrandom samples cannot be used to estimate population characteristics or behavior. In other words, you cannot make percentage, average or other quantitative estimates with non-random samples. However, you can get "indications," "initial evaluations" and "tentative responses" to your questions or stimuli.

Sometimes nonrandom samples cannot be avoided. Populations may be difficult to reach, and time and money may be tight. You may need to use convenient locations to find the right kinds of people, say coffee shops to do muffin taste tests. Just be careful not to assume your results represent the entire market.

CAN I USE VOLUNTEERS?

Be careful using volunteers because they are also nonrandom. Problems can arise from *self-selection*, where respondents themselves choose to be in the study. This happens when someone picks up a questionnaire from a table in a public place, readers mail in a questionnaire stuck inside a magazine, or Internet users who visit Yahoo participate in a poll. Volunteers may participate more than once, they may have strong feelings about the topic or they may have nothing better to do, so avoid volunteers if possible.

CHAPTER 19

HOW TO SAMPLE

I f you decide to use a sample rather than a census, it's not just a matter of arbitrarily picking a sampling technique. You have to know your population, your sample size, and then find a list that represents the population.

The sampling technique is also important. Random samples are representative of the population and you can calculate sampling error and use other statistics (see Chapter 20). Nonrandom samples are not representative and cannot be used to make quantitative estimates to the population but they can be useful for qualitative studies.

THE FRAME

The list from which you select your sample is called a *frame*. It is important to distinguish between populations and frames. Not every population has a frame — people who play Mahjong or those who work in the underground economy may be difficult to enumerate, and some frames are notoriously bad in representing the population. For example, most telephone books are poor frames because unlisted numbers are missing.

There can be several different frames for the same population. The white pages contain just listed residential numbers, but all possible 7-digit numbers contain all residential numbers (along with all businesses, government, and other phone numbers). Frames can have errors. A printed version of the *Broadcasting and*

Table 19.1
POPULATIONS AND FRAMES

Population	Frame
Telephone numbers	Telephone books
Telephone numbers	All possible 7-digit numbers
Addresses	City Clerk list of addresses
Employees	Employee records printout
Television stations	*Broadcasting and Cable Yearbook*
Voters	County Clerk's list of voters, last primary election
Voters	County Clerk's voter registration list
Public relations practitioners	PRSA member list
Public relations practitioners	IABC member list

Cable Yearbook would not contain new radio stations. An online version would be better. You need to secure a frame that is as reasonably accurate as possible for your study. Table 19.1 shows a small list of populations and frames.

Sometimes frames are difficult to locate or create. As an example, Arbitron Radio Ratings wanted to contact radio sales account executives, but there was no directory listing them. So Arbitron went through a complicated process to generate a frame that considered the percentage of population in each market segment, contacted stations in each segment, and called each station to elicit names of account executives (full details are at Arbitron's Web page, a free report, "What Are Your Salespeople Thinking?").

RANDOM NUMBERS

If human decisions are assumed to be biased, how can humans select random samples? They cannot. So we eliminate human bias in deciding which members to select for the sample by using a random number table or a random number generator on a computer.

Almost every academic book on research methods has a random number table, but you can also generate your own table by using your PC's spreadsheet.

There are two important steps: use a different location on the table for each sample, and, when generating a random table on your PC, do not use the same "seed" twice. The functions RAND and RANDBETWEEN are useful, and recalculation causes new numbers to be produced. Using Quattro and the function "@RANDBETWEEN(0,9)" in each cell, my spreadsheet produced the random number table shown in Table 19.2.

How do you use the table? You can start anywhere as long as you don't start in the same place twice. If you need ten one-digit numbers you could start top left, going down the column (0, 3, 4,...) or you could start in the lower left and go up (2, 0, 7, ...).

If you need ten three-digit numbers between zero and 200, use three columns. Skip over the numbers that are out of range (over 200) and skip duplicates. If you start top left, use the first three columns. You get "033, 362, 466, 248, 107, 401, 826..." The usable numbers are "033, 107, 120, 139, 199, 037, 148, 130, 028, 018" (the rest are out of range). When you get to the bottom of the table and need more numbers, return to the top of the next three columns and go down again (501, 701, 599, etc., with usable numbers being 018, 121, etc.).

RANDOM SAMPLING TECHNIQUES

There are many ways to sample. The most commonly used are simple random, systematic random, stratified, cluster and random digit dialing (RDD). The type you select depends on what you need to sample, the size of your sample (usually designated N), the size of the frame, and expectations about the population.

The simple random sampling technique is most useful for short lists or small frames. These include small populations like companies with a small number of employees, schools with only a few hundred students, small clubs, local membership in the Chamber of Commerce for small cities, etc. Simple random sampling can also be useful when you need to randomly order a list such as a scale for a questionnaire or anytime you need to make a random decision. The steps are easy.

1. Number the list/frame.
2. Determine the sample size (N).
3. Select N random numbers.
4. Go back to the list/frame and select those from the list matching the random numbers.

Table 19.2
RANDOM NUMBER TABLE

0	3	3	5	0	1	3	2	5	2	2	8	5	1	1	0
3	6	2	7	0	1	4	9	0	9	0	5	0	9	8	0
4	6	6	5	9	9	0	9	0	8	5	6	9	7	7	1
2	4	8	0	1	8	3	1	9	6	8	7	4	6	3	8
1	0	7	6	2	5	8	4	0	2	0	2	3	2	6	1
4	0	1	4	1	5	9	5	6	7	1	1	3	7	0	4
8	2	6	6	9	8	2	0	9	6	8	0	5	6	9	8
8	3	5	7	1	2	0	4	9	2	3	3	8	1	9	3
3	5	8	1	2	1	1	6	2	5	4	0	4	9	1	0
9	2	0	3	4	6	1	4	6	3	6	3	4	8	1	3
9	9	9	4	8	2	3	2	5	0	0	3	0	1	6	9
7	0	2	2	0	5	3	0	9	9	9	4	9	7	6	6
7	9	6	2	2	5	9	7	9	1	7	5	3	8	8	8
9	4	4	0	3	9	7	3	6	3	3	5	7	5	6	8
7	1	9	0	8	7	5	6	4	3	3	8	6	5	0	4
9	7	5	0	9	0	3	0	7	2	6	3	9	1	6	3
1	2	0	0	2	3	0	3	4	4	9	3	4	9	7	2
8	0	7	3	3	6	5	0	3	5	1	0	8	3	4	0
8	7	5	6	1	5	3	6	9	2	7	1	5	7	4	0
5	5	3	9	7	6	2	2	8	0	7	5	8	1	2	4
5	7	1	9	3	2	2	6	3	9	6	3	5	2	2	7
8	6	3	3	5	7	9	1	2	3	5	7	3	9	1	8
3	8	0	2	3	3	4	2	6	2	6	4	8	9	6	7
5	9	9	5	9	9	3	2	0	6	9	2	0	0	8	2
2	2	2	1	2	5	2	5	8	7	9	3	9	3	3	6
6	8	2	2	3	7	7	3	9	8	3	6	4	7	9	2
2	3	9	3	5	4	6	9	5	9	4	3	5	2	2	3
4	2	1	7	2	3	3	6	3	1	7	5	6	7	6	1
8	5	6	0	2	0	6	0	8	2	1	1	4	2	4	6
1	3	9	6	5	4	3	1	7	1	3	4	5	4	9	4
2	3	5	1	4	5	5	4	1	3	8	2	0	2	6	7
1	9	9	8	9	6	2	7	1	8	5	1	8	9	6	5
8	4	7	2	2	8	1	4	2	2	0	6	2	0	5	5
0	3	7	2	4	8	8	2	4	2	9	7	8	2	8	1
6	6	5	3	8	6	6	0	6	6	4	0	9	1	6	3
9	2	0	5	6	5	2	4	9	9	6	9	4	8	3	3
5	6	4	1	8	4	9	4	1	6	3	2	8	1	8	4
8	1	6	3	0	3	0	5	5	9	2	2	8	1	8	8
1	4	8	3	5	6	5	1	0	0	6	3	5	0	4	9
7	7	5	7	1	6	0	5	6	2	2	0	1	4	3	1
8	7	1	4	3	5	0	9	6	4	9	9	2	7	3	9
9	5	2	5	4	3	0	9	0	6	8	2	7	7	0	1
2	8	3	1	2	5	0	4	6	9	2	7	8	3	7	9
1	3	0	6	5	1	8	5	2	4	6	9	4	4	9	6
6	1	3	1	1	6	6	6	8	0	8	3	5	8	8	3
7	3	6	4	3	3	6	2	3	0	5	0	8	3	6	2
0	2	8	0	7	4	9	4	5	3	1	9	7	2	8	7
7	9	7	7	7	5	2	2	0	7	3	5	9	2	0	2
0	1	8	3	6	2	5	2	2	4	9	1	4	5	4	3
2	2	2	9	3	2	8	6	2	1	7	0	3	4	4	4

JOEY REAGAN

Suppose you are doing a qualitative internal communication study for which you want to randomly select 10 employees, and your company has 100 employees. Following the steps listed above, you would:

1. Number the list of employees from 001 to 100.
   - 001 Arthur A. Abrams
   - 002 Bradley B. Anderson
   - 002 John B. Buchannan
     - •
     - •
     - •
   - 100 Joey Zygote
2. Determine the sample size, $N = 10$.
3. Select ten three-digit numbers from the random number table. Notice that the numbers must be between 001 and 100. Starting in a different place than before, lower right and going up, you get 049, 055, 082, and so on (others are out of range).
4. Go back to the employee list and select employees 49, 55, 82, etc.

Simple random samples can also be used to make random decisions. If you want to randomly order 20 items in a questionnaire, you select 20 random numbers between 0 and 20 and place the items in that order. If you want to select two "winners" out of 50 employees who want to move to two new offices, select two random numbers between 1 and 50.

Simple random samples can be time-consuming and tedious for large frames or samples. Imagine working with a printed list of 25,000 members of a worldwide association and trying to generate a sample of $N = 300$ going back and forth between the random number table and the list. So for large populations and frames, you need to turn to more efficient methods of drawing samples.

Systematic-random sampling involves the use of a system to make the task easier while maintaining a random component to give each item an equal chance of being selected. The most common systematic sampling procedure is to take the "Nth" item on a list with the following steps.

1. Get a frame total T.
2. Decide on the sample size N.
3. Divide T/N for the skip interval I.
4. Select a random start point S between 1 and I.
5. Start at S, then go to S+I, S+2I, S+3I, etc. throughout the frame.

Let's go back to the example above where you are doing a qualitative internal communication study, only this time your company has 4,000 employees, and you want a random sample of $N = 100$. You could simply take every 40th employee, but don't arbitrarily select employee 40, employee 80, employee 120, etc. Instead, follow the systematic random procedure:

1. Frame total, $T = 4,000$
2. Sample size, $N = 100$
3. Find the skip interval by dividing $T/N = I = 40$.
4. Select a two-digit random start point. In Table 19.2 start at columns seven and eight on top. The first two-digit random number between 1 and 40 is 32.
5. Select employee 32, employee $32+40 = 72$, employee $32+80 = 112$, etc.

A second method is to use a system to select from pages on a list or frame. Many frames come in pages: business directories, phone directories, even computer screens of employee names. As long as each page has an equal number of addresses or phone numbers per page, a simple method is to divide the sample size by the number of pages to get the number of items to select per page. Within the page, use the systematic random process described above.

You have to be clever if you have a partial number of items per page. For example, if you had 5.5 names per page that obviously won't work. If you need 11 every two pages, you could select six on one page and five on another, randomly selecting which pages (odd or even) get six names.

Using the above example of an employee study, suppose a computer printout of all employee names had 40 pages with 50 names per page and you wanted $N = 200$.

1. Names selected per page, ($N = 200/40$ pages, or 5 names per page)
2. Select five random numbers between 1 and 50 (50 names/page)
3. Starting at the bottom left of Table 19.2. Go up. The random numbers are 22, 01, 02, 13, 28 (others are out of range)
4. Go to each page:
   a. Page 1, select employees 22, 01, 02, 13, 28
   b. Page 2, select employees 22, 01, 02, 13, 28
   c. And so on for each page

Systematic randomization can also work for the process of selecting participants by interviewers. (If you have ever watched some interviewers at malls, they tend to avoid the weird-looking people, poor people and others who still might be in your target.) You could randomly select times to interview throughout the

JOEY REAGAN

week, avoiding bias against people who only shop at certain times or days; randomly select entrances, eliminating bias against people who always enter from other doors; and randomly determine how many people go by before the interviewer takes the next shopper, avoiding selection bias. What is important is that there is an equal chance for each person to be in the sample.

There is one potential problem when using systematic samples: biased frames. Suppose that in the employee list the first name on each page is a supervisor. If random number "1" was not selected then supervisors would be eliminated from the sample. If "1" was selected then all supervisors would be represented. To solve this, just select separate samples for each group (a form of stratified sampling).

The *stratified sampling* technique is used to guarantee representation to various segments (strata) of the population, like trying to get an even split between males and females in the sample or trying to proportion the sample for geographic divisions. Stratification can take place during the sampling process if the appropriate information is available, or it can take place during an interview.

Assume that a city makes up 40 percent of the population of a county. You would make sure that your original sample is proportionally selected to represent that split — that is, 40 percent from the city and 60 percent from rural areas — and you would monitor how many interviews were being completed for each geographic area as the study progressed.

Other stratification issues include trying to get proportional representation for important demographics like gender and income. At the beginning of an interview you could get roughly a 50/50 split for gender by alternately asking for a male or female to interview (randomly selecting which to ask for first, of course). Or you could ask questions when opening the interview to determine demographic characteristics of respondents. You would interview those who fit the demographics you need.

Cluster sampling uses groups of the population for the frame rather than individual members of the population. This technique is used when you either cannot get a frame that represents the population or there are practical reasons for using groups. Suppose you were doing personal interviews within households across a large city. Using a sample of addresses might require interviewers to travel long distances, hence, travel and time costs of interviewing would skyrocket. However, using geographic clusters would minimize travel time and expense.

Multi-stage sampling is often used with clusters. This involves sampling clusters within clusters rather than including all units in one large cluster. For example, suppose you initially sampled census tracts. You could randomly select the household to interview by doing the following:

1. Randomly select a block of houses in the tract.
2. Randomly decide which side of the street to interview.
3. Number the house on that side of the street and randomly select the houses to visit.

Random digit dialing (RDD) overcomes the problem of unlisted numbers because all possible digits or numbers are available. RDD uses random numbers to fill in the last four digits of a phone number. This means that all numbers, including unlisted, have a chance to be in the sample.

RDD enhances simple random sampling. You just need to know the "density" or proportion of telephone numbers in each exchange (the first three numbers) along with the sample size. The following example uses only three exchanges, but the principle can be extended to large cities with multiple exchanges and even several area codes.

1. Obtain the density for the exchanges. Assume the exchanges are 372, 335, 489 and the densities are:

   a. 372 - 20 percent of all residential numbers
   b. 335 - 40 percent of all residential numbers
   c. 489 - 40 percent of all residential numbers

2. Assume a sample of $N = 200$; thus:

   a. 372 = 20 percent of the of the sample = 40 phone numbers
   b. 335 = 40 percent of the of the sample = 80 phone numbers
   c. 489 = 40 percent of the of the sample = 80 phone numbers

3. Select 200 four-digit random numbers and add to the exchanges

372-6642	335-7636	489-9807
372-4529	335-2490	489-8782
372-3715	335-4289	489-4936
Up to 40 nos.	Up to 80 nos.	Up to 80 nos.

There are problems with RDD. You get a lot of junk numbers (business numbers and nonworking numbers) and the exchanges cover areas outside your target population. Sampling services (Survey Sampling International, Scientific Telephone Samples, and others) solve these problems by screening out most of the junk numbers. In addition, these services can provide samples that are difficult to obtain. They can provide:

- RDD samples cleaned of numbers not in your target area, businesses and other junk to guarantee 90 percent usable numbers
- E-mail address samples
- Global samples
- Targeted samples, screened for age, income and other characteristics

Of course, there is a cost involved. My lowest cost for a statewide RDD sample was $700, and the cost can increase depending on the size and parameters associated with your sample.

RANDOMLY SAMPLING CONTENT

Suppose you cannot afford the time or money to monitor all of your competitors' advertising or all media coverage of your company. How can you get an accurate representation?

You should be able to find some sampling method that can get you a good selection. For instance, if you want to monitor CNN coverage of your company, you could randomly select times and days to record. Just make sure you avoid selecting the same time each day.

NONRANDOM SAMPLING

Most qualitative studies do not use random samples. Usually participants are recruited with the breadth of possible responses in mind, because the point is to generate ideas rather than percentages of the population. So you need respondents who offer a variety of perspectives, both negative and positive opinions, both experienced and inexperienced, rich and poor, and so on.

Convenience samples find respondents where it's convenient, such as malls, meeting halls, community centers, religious buildings, work sites, schools, markets and so on. These samples are useful for initial testing of ideas or pretesting questionnaires and a study's methods.

Judgment sampling is based on your judgment as a researcher. You simply select sample members because you think they are appropriate. For example, you might walk out on the street and ask passers-by if they ski. You then ask your skiing questions of those who say "yes." This technique is useful for getting some initial qualitative responses, such as pretesting questionnaires for readability.

Quota sampling starts at the beginning of a list and stops when a certain size is attained. It is often used for subgroup quotas like stratified samples, but without the randomness. For example, you could start at the beginning of the phonebook and interview people until you complete 200 interviews, and within that sample you could stop interviewing females when you reach 100, stop interviewing males when you reach 100.

Snowball samples are based on the recommendations of the initial people you interview. These samples can be heavily biased because subsequent interviewees are likely to be similar to your initial interviewees. However, if you just need to interview similar people to do some qualitative work — say you want to talk with model train enthusiasts — then you can ask your first interviewee to recommend others with the same interest in model trains.

Volunteer samples are similar to convenience samples except respondents choose to volunteer in response to a general invitation for participation. For example, you could post a questionnaire on the Internet and place links on various Web pages inviting participation, or you could place piles of questionnaires in public places — coffee shops, cafeterias, government licensing offices and so on — with a public sign asking people to fill out and return them.

CHAPTER 20

SAMPLING ERROR AND SAMPLE SIZE

Most data in communication research come from samples. For example, if a poll says a congressional candidate is 6 percentage points ahead of the nearest challenger, then many people think the candidates are actually that far apart. However, if you pay attention to media reports of polls, you will often see, "The margin of error is plus or minus three percentage points." That's *sampling error*, or to state it more generally, all numbers from samples are estimates and all samples are subject to sampling error.

Sampling error is inextricably linked to sample size. There are several factors that determine the appropriate sample size. These include what sampling error you will accept and what percentage of the sample responds. The size of the sample relates to how accurate estimates are of the population.

The few calculations presented in this chapter are those most basic to all sample-based studies. In the formulas below, the assumption is that large samples are used, those above 200, so that calculations can be simplified without using statistical correction factors. In addition, the calculations are for percentages. There are slightly different calculations for averages, available in other research texts.

These calculations also assume random samples, so studies done with convenience samples, volunteers and other nonrandom methods, even if the nonrandom sample sizes are large, must not employ these calculations.

CONFIDENCE LEVEL AND CONFIDENCE INTERVAL

Samples are not perfect. Remember, the results are only estimates and we can never be 100 percent sure of them.

So statisticians estimate sampling error, and they do using two criteria. The first is *confidence level,* which is a probability associated with the estimates we obtain. If we say our confidence level is 95 percent, that means the probability is 95 times out of 100 that the results we obtain from a sample are reasonably accurate, within plus or minus a certain percentage. The probability is that you are right 19 times out of 20, and that's a good bet. It's a lot better than flipping a coin or guessing. While other confidence levels can be used, it is a common rule of thumb to use 95 percent in social science .

The second criterion is *confidence interval,* which gives an estimate of the accuracy of a number obtained in the study. It is that "plus or minus three percentage points" that polls refer to. It is a range of values around the estimate. It is an interval such as 32 percent ± 3 percent, or between 29 percent and 35 percent. "Confidence interval" and "sampling error" are equivalent terms, so they are often used interchangeably.

Confidence level and interval are related to each other such that we have a probability that our estimate is within a certain range of values. For example, rather than thinking that a number from research is exact, you should think, "I am XX percent confident (confidence level) that the true value in the population is the estimate plus or minus XX percent (confidence interval)." Suppose you conducted a survey of 300 St. Louis residents and found that 64 percent had visited the Gateway Arch. You would conclude, "I am 95 percent sure that the true percentage of all residents who have visited Gateway Arch is 64 percent ±5.4 percent or somewhere between 58.6 percent and 69.4 percent."

The calculations below are based on a 95 percent confidence level. That is where the "1.96" in the calculation comes from. The formulas are based on the "normal curve" from Chapter 17. Remember that 95 percent of the area under the curve is between ±1.96 standard deviations.

SAMPLING ERROR

Remembering that research based on samples is not perfect — just an accurate reflection of the population — you should ask, "How accurate is it, anyway?" When polls are reported on TV or in newspapers with "an error of plus or minus three points," you may have wondered, "How do they come up with that number?" The answer is they use sampling error.

Maximum sampling error (SE_{max}) is calculated before you do your study, when all you know is the sample size. Once you have selected the sample size, you can calculate the maximum sampling error before you have collected data. This is important because you need to know if the confidence interval is small enough or accurate enough for your needs. Let's say you are working on a close political campaign. If your sampling error is too large, you won't be able to differentiate between your candidate's support and the support for the opponent.

Where N = sample size, for percentages the formula is:

$$SE_{max} = \pm 1.96 \sqrt{\frac{.25}{N}}$$

If you had a sample size of $N = 300$, the maximum error is:

$$SE_{max} = \pm 1.96 \sqrt{\frac{.25}{300}}$$

$$SE_{max} = \pm .057$$

Or, to convert this proportion to a percentage, multiply by 100:

$$SE_{max} = \pm 5.7\%$$

This means that you can expect the maximum sampling error for any estimate in your upcoming study to be ± 5.7 percent. If the error is too high, you can increase your sample size to reduce the error. If you decide that you can't afford a larger sample, then you can choose to accept the higher error or abandon the study.

In contrast to maximum sampling error is *sampling error* (SE) which is calculated when you have finished your project and have specific estimates for which you want to know the error.

Say you are interested in the demographics of your market because your advertisers want to target households with incomes over $75,000. You conducted a survey and found that 9.4 percent of your sample have incomes over $75,000. You calculate the sampling error with the following formula (since "p" is the proportion estimate, make sure you change percentages to proportions, 9.4 percent = .094):

$$SE = \pm 1.96 \sqrt{\frac{p \times q}{N}}$$

where:

p = proportion estimate
q = 1−p
N = sample size

If your sample size was $N = 200$, you can calculate the error for the estimate as:

p = .094 (9.4 percent converted to proportion)
q = (1−p) = (1−.094) = .906

$$SE = \pm 1.96 \sqrt{\frac{.094 \times .906}{200}}$$

SE = ± .040

SE = ± 4.0%

What does this calculation mean? It means we are 95 percent confident that the true population value, the percentage of people in the population with incomes above $75,000 falls within the sampling error. We have a low probability of being wrong. In this example it means:

- We are 95 percent sure that the true population value falls within a range of numbers, 9.4 percent ± 4.0 percent.
- We are very confident that the true population value is somewhere between 5.4 percent and 13.4 percent.

Does the size of the population matter? No! It is the size of the sample that matters. Notice that the formula ignores population size, once the population rises above a couple thousand, it is only the sample size that affects sampling error.

RESEARCH IS AN ACCURATE APPROXIMATION

The calculations show that you should keep several "guidelines" in mind about how you will interpret the results. Research provides estimates; research is not 100 percent accurate; and samples reflect the population within a range of values.

Although research is a good bet (95 percent confidence is much better than a coin flip), there is always a chance you can be wrong. You should not risk your entire budget on one roll of the dice — or one survey. In the long run, you should come out ahead if you are regularly using representative research. With proper sampling techniques the odds are 95 percent in your favor!

EXAMPLE OF SAMPLING ERROR APPLICATION

After a campaign to develop trust in your company, you conduct a study in which you find that 55 percent of your target have high trust in your company and 44 percent have high trust in your competitor. That's an 11 percentage-point difference. It seems like a lot. But are you sure you are really ahead of your competition? Remember sampling error and perform the simple calculations. Consider the following results if you used a sample size of $N = 250$:

- Your company: 55 percent say they have high trust in you.
  - Sampling error: ± 6.2 percent.
  - Range of values (confidence interval): 48.8 percent to 61.2 percent.
- Competitor: 44 percent say they have high trust in your competitor.
  - Sampling error: ± 6.2 percent.
  - Range of values (confidence interval): 37.8 percent to 50.2 percent.

Compare the confidence intervals (sampling errors) for your company and your competitor. They overlap. It's *possible* that the true population values are as high as 50.2 percent for your competitor and as low as 48.8 percent for you. Your campaign might have failed. Of course, the true numbers could be anywhere in the range, and you could have succeeded even more strongly, but you will not know for sure on the basis of one study. Thus, the need for replication.

SELECTING SAMPLE SIZES

Selecting an appropriate sample size can be puzzling. Very small samples are quite useless for making population estimates because they have large error — a sample size of 50 has an error of ± 13.9 percent. Even with a sample size of $N = 200$, the sampling error might seem large (± 6.9 percent). Obviously, you see a negative relation between sample size and sampling error, but are bigger samples always better? Here are some maximum errors for different sample sizes:

- $N = 100, \pm 9.8\%$
- $N = 200, \pm 6.9\%$
- $N = 400, \pm 4.9\%$
- $N = 800, \pm 3.5\%$
- $N = 1600, \pm 2.5\%$

Notice that *as sample size increases, sampling error decreases*, but bigger is not always better because the relationship is not linear. That is, when you double sample size, the error does not decrease by one half. You have to *quadruple* the sample size to cut the error in half. This is illustrated in Figure 20.1.

Close to the Y-axis (the vertical axis), the samples are under 100 and have large sampling errors. As the samples get bigger, the errors fall dramatically until about $N = 200$ to 300 where the curve flattens out. It then takes very large increases in the sample size just to get small decreases in the error. So, all thing equal, the best sample size is around 300. This is the point at which the costs of data collection (both time and money) and reduction in error are reasonable. Above that, the costs steeply increase without much change in error.

There are special cases when large samples are needed. For example, ratings services may use $N = 600$ for local market studies, but this is because the sample may need to be split into smaller pieces. Ratings usually involve multiple counties, but a local advertiser may only care about a single county that uses only a part of the overall sample. Academicians also have needs for very large samples, such as 25-year panel studies that will have a large number of dropouts and studies that require the sample to be broken down into very small subsets.

OVERSAMPLING

If the sampling method you used was perfect and if everyone cooperated, then you would just select the sample size to match the error you are willing to accept. However, the reality is that no sample is perfect. You will get some business numbers (even with RDD), people refuse to cooperate, some phone numbers are discontinued, addresses don't exist, the weather is good and no one is home, and so on. So you will need to *oversample*, which is merely selecting additional members of the sample to account for those problems.

If you want to interview 300 people over the telephone, you will need to draw more than 300 phone numbers. How much you oversample depends on the *expected completion rate*, the proportion of the sample that completes the survey. If you want to end up with a sample of $N = 300$ telephone numbers, divide N by the expected completion rate. Increase your sample by another 50 percent (multiply by 1.5) just

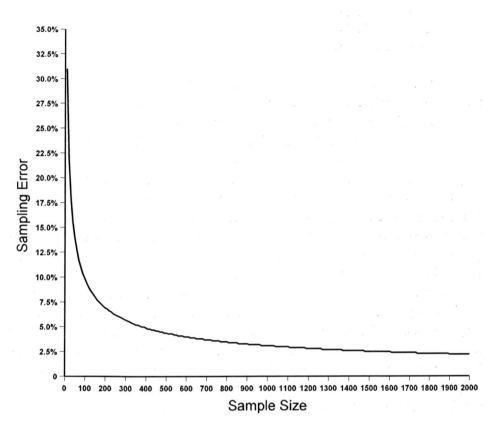

Figure 20.1
THE RELATION OF SAMPLING ERROR TO SAMPLE SIZE

to be sure. If you expect a phone survey to have a completion rate of 45 percent, then for $N = 300$:

$$\text{Sample Size} = \frac{\text{Desired completion } (N)}{\text{Expected completion rate}} \times 1.5$$

$$\text{Sample size} = \frac{N = 300}{.45} \times 1.5 = 1000$$

How do you know what the expected completion rate is? You have to get information about the market or area in which you are doing research. Talk with others who have done the same type of research in your market (sampling services are good sources) because response rates and problems vary from market to market.

CHAPTER 21

RESEARCH ADMINISTRATION

Administration of research includes actions from your research director or consultant as well as from yourself in order to ensure that the projects you commission are conducted appropriately and honestly.

To ensure the integrity and accuracy of your study, it is not enough to hire a consultant, employ people to do telephone interviews, or tell your research department to do your study. You should not assume they will follow your directions. This is not out of a sense of distrust but out of a sense of professional responsibility. Honest people can make mistakes or get complacent. What I recommend are standard practices in the research industry.

BE ORGANIZED AND PRE-TEST

Being organized and pretesting keeps you on top of your study and eliminates many errors. You must be organized on all steps of the research process. This includes having a timeline for your study (see Table 21.1). You create one or expect your consultant to provide one.

Make sure your timeline includes time for pretesting. That means calling some real people on the phone or having them fill out your mail questionnaires or running in an auditorium to make sure the sound works and the monitors are viewable. There will always be something to fix. A question will need to be reworded simply because telephone technology is so bad that words can't be under-

Table 21.1
TIMELINE FOR A TELEPHONE SURVEY

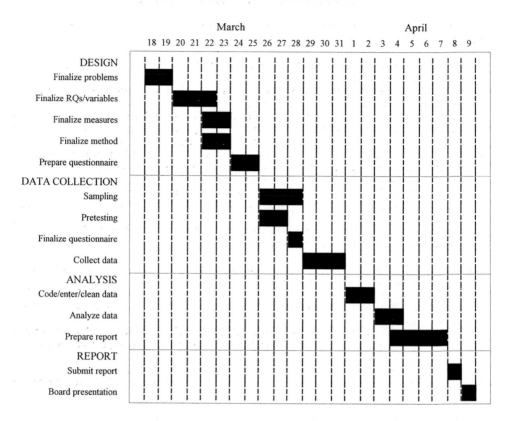

stood, or someone will write down "all day" when you wanted a number of hours, or you need a different audio cable in the auditorium.

STANDARDIZATION

Standardization assures that the data you collect are all based on the same stimulus. Imagine the different responses you get to, "What do you think about XYZ Company?" vs. "Is XYZ doing a good job? Why?" In other words, you want to ensure that each person is asked the same question, in the same way, in the same order. Thus, any differences are due to differences in the population, not differences in your procedures. In addition, standardization allows others to replicate your study by using the same questions or stimuli.

Always train your personnel. If you hire a vendor or subcontractor to do part

Table 21.2
TELEPHONE INTERVIEWER INSTRUCTIONS

TELEPHONE INTERVIEWER INSTRUCTIONS

1. Allow the phone to ring 3 times before calling it "no answer." Call back answering machines next day. After the next complete, call b ck a busy.
2. Material in ALL CAPS is directions, etc. DO NOT read the material in ALL CAPS to the respondent.
3. Avoid "uh-huh," "ok," "that's right," etc. Do not coach the respondent.
4. Read the questionnaire exactly as printed. Do not alter the wording or question order.
5. If the respondent wants verification of the legitimacy of the study, they may speak to the supervisor, or they may call Joey Reagan at 555-6666 during the day, or Dr. Reagan can call them back.
6. If a respondent wants to know more about the study, ask them to answer the questions first so we don't bias their answers. If they want to know who is sponsoring the survey, say: "It's a study of media use and shopping conducted by Reagan Market Research."
7. If a respondent has difficulty with answers, ask for their "best estimate."
8. If the respondent says they don't have time, make an appointment to call later or on another day. Ask, "What is a better time to call?"
9. If the respondent wants to know how long the interview will take, say "about five minutes."
10. Always be courteous! Even if the respondent doesn't want to cooperate. Remember, they can refuse to answer any question at any time.
11. If a respondent does not understand a question, try repeating the question. You may try to clarify but NEVER reveal an answer that's in ALL CAPS.
12. If there are problems using the CATI, problems entering responses, problems with routing, typing in responses, other problems, write down the responses on the notepad and notify your supervisor as soon as you can.
13. For each question the respondent should have heard, there should be an answer entered. If not we will assume you did not ask the question and you will be warned. After two warnings you will be dismissed for the third error.
14. Show partial completes to your supervisor. Add GENDER to partial completes.
15. Your interviews will be verified. You will be supervised while calling, including audio monitoring of your interviews.

- You will be assigned a partner to role-play the interview before starting work.
- If you have any problems or questions call Joey Reagan (555-6666).

of your study, you or they must train interviewers in a consistent manner. The procedures for conducting an interview must be standardized, so training includes written instructions (see Figure 21.2 for telephone interviewer instructions). Note that these instructions provide standardization for what constitutes a "no answer," dealing with busy signals, how to read the questionnaire, how to deal with respondent questions, etc. Besides going over these procedures with interviewers, they should receive face-to-face training so they have the chance to ask questions, and they should role-play the interviews on the phone so they do not make mistakes by starting their first few interviews cold. Procedures also should be written for other techniques, such as a script of what experimenters say to subjects.

Table 21.3
FOCUS GROUP BILL OF RIGHTS
(Used by permission of Tom Greenbaum, Groups Plus, Inc.)

The Focus Group Bill Of Rights
By Tom Greenbaum

The Client's Rights

- To retain a moderator who is an experienced and competent professional in focus group research.
- To know who will conduct the groups and who will be writing the report before signing the contract with the research company.
- To receive a discussion guide well in advance of the groups in order to provide input to the moderator relative to modifications.
- To agree to all recruitment specifications and to review a copy of the recruitment screening questionnaire before participants are asked to come to the groups.
- To be provided with a one-page summary of the participants (without last names, addresses, or phone numbers as per the QRCA Code of Ethics) in each session with key screening criteria identified.
- To be provided with a formal, written report of the groups on or before the date agreed upon.
- To be provided with information about the various research Codes of Ethics (QRCA, CMOR, RIC) with respect to respondent confidentiality and respect.
- To have full groups of qualified participants who arrive on time at the facility, understanding that there will be some exceptions.

The Respondent's Rights

- To be told the general content of the discussion to preclude them participating in a subject about which they would not feel comfortable.
- To be told about video or audio taping of sessions and the presence of people observing the sessions from behind the one-way mirror.
- To be paid for coming to the groups in the event they are not selected for participation, presuming they arrived at the facility within ten minutes of the agreed upon starting time.
- To be treated with dignity and respect by the personnel at the facility and those conducting the research in the room and behind the mirror.
- To receive light food and beverages consistent with the time of day the groups are held.
- To have the right to withdraw or not answer any question or sample any product at any time.
- To be assured of confidentiality; that is, that their names, addresses, phone numbers or personal information will not be released to clients or anyone else without their permission.

While the above emphasizes the details for a quantitative study, qualitative studies must follow a similar system: being organized, pretesting, having a timetable and so on. Instead of interviewer instructions, a focus group might have a set of instructions like the "Bill of Rights" shown in Table 21.3 (Note: This is an abbreviated version. The original also includes "Facilities' Rights" and "Moderator's Rights.")

JOEY REAGAN

PROPRIETARY RESEARCH

While most academic research is available to the public, commercial research is kept secret because you do not want your competitors to know about your study or to get the results that you have paid good money for. This is called *proprietary research*. This should be stressed to all involved in the project. A rumor that research is underway gives your competitors important information. Also letting people know they may be interviewed — such as your employees or the general public — may predispose them to think about their answers and, thus, create some bias.

When you draw people from outside your company into the project, it should be made clear that the project is secret. This is a normal practice for data collection firms. But since they often employ temporary or part-time interviewers, or you may hire someone temporarily for data entry or clerking assistance, it is essential to complete a secrecy agreement, such as the following:

SECRECY AGREEMENT

The nature of this study, sponsors, questions, data, telephone numbers, sampling procedures and all other information about this study are confidential. This study and the data are the property of RMR — Reagan Market Research or its clients. Revealing any of this information will subject you to liability for any loss due to its disclosure.

NAME (print): _____

SIGNATURE: _____

DATE: _____

KEEPING TRACK OF DATA COLLECTION

It is important to keep track of the progress of your study so you know if it's proceeding according to schedule or if there are any problems with the sample or procedures. Below is a *call sheet* for a telephone survey. You could use it, for example, to list your RDD sample. If you purchase a sample, the numbers come in an electronic file that you can copy to your CATI system or into your call sheet template.

The call sheet is the basis for calculating what proportion of your sample refused the interview, completed the interview, were junk numbers and so on, so you can compute *response rate* (see Chapter 23). These numbers are important so you can make sure data collection is on schedule (completing enough each day?), track problems with the questionnaire or procedures (too many refusals?), determine whether the sample you purchased from the sampling service is useful (too much junk?) and other issues.

TELEPHONE CALL SHEET

INTERVIEWER:_____ DATE:_____

Phone number   CIRCLE Status

_____ CM RF BUS DIS CB:_____ OTH:_____
_____ CM RF BUS DIS CB:_____ OTH:_____
_____ CM RF BUS DIS CB:_____ OTH:_____
_____ CM RF BUS DIS CB:_____ OTH:_____
_____ CM RF BUS DIS CB:_____ OTH:_____
_____ CM RF BUS DIS CB:_____ OTH:_____
_____ CM RF BUS DIS CB:_____ OTH:_____

CM = Complete RF = Refused BUS = Business
DIS = Disconnected/out of service
CB = Call back, write in time/day to call back OTH = Other
NOTE: Mark final status. E.g., If a CB is completed, circle CM.

A similar sheet can be used for a mail survey with addresses instead of telephone numbers, and check-offs for when questionnaires were mailed out, whether they were returned by the deadline, when reminders were sent, and when follow-ups were sent. Other techniques should have similar progress sheets.

MONITORING THE STUDY

Staying on top of your project means not just being organized and pretesting your procedures. It also means keeping people "honest."

I put "honest" in quotes because most people don't deliberately cheat, but most perform better if they are trained and then supervised. So keep track of how things are going. If there are four evenings of phone interviewing, you should keep yourself informed of how the project is doing each evening. If you have a consultant, they should inform you of this. You need to listen to people doing the interviewing. Reputable data collection firms will allow you to call in and be switched over to monitor interviews in progress. If it's a mail survey, check the envelopes. Are they addressed correctly? Are the stamps sloppy? How are questionnaires being coded?

When it comes to data analysis you should copy the data file into your spreadsheet even if you won't do the final analysis. It just gives you a feel for how the interviews went, how people were answering and how the results will "look." You should try running some data analysis yourself. Simple results — percentages, averages and simple crosstabulations — in your spreadsheet are easy. Do you get the same numbers as are in the report?

Verification is an essential part of monitoring. That means contacting a small subsample of those who were allegedly interviewed to make sure the calls were actually done or someone actually showed up for the personal interview. This ensures that the data in your data file are accurate. It's not just the $25,000 you want returned if there are faked interviews. You especially don't want to make bad decisions based on faulty data.

SAVE YOUR PRODUCT

Do not be satisfied with only a copy of the final report. Keep a copy of the data file and the codebook (a listing of all the questions, response categories and coding used for data entry) and questionnaires, lists of procedures, stimuli such as videos, scripts, etc. This is vital because three weeks from now or six months from now you may have a question that wasn't analyzed for the report, or a year from now you may want to replicate your study and compare the new results with the old.

CHAPTER 22

DEALING WITH DATA

Y ou have gathered data and are now at the point where you'd like to do some analysis. However, there is another step before conducting analyses. This step takes the data you have collected and checks for errors in data entry and makes sure they are in a form usable for analysis.

DATA ENTRY

Some of your data will be entered directly into a computer file if you use a CATI system. However, responses on mail questionnaires, some personal interviews, and other techniques will require you to transfer those responses into a computer file. For example, you'll need to transfer those "1 = yes" and "2 = no" from paper questionnaires to your computers. This is usually done with a spreadsheet. You may also have open-ended responses or verbatims to enter, usually into a word processing file, or you may want to code open-ends into categories.

Coding is the process of turning responses into numbers. Some are obvious, "1 = yes"; others are not, such as, "I think they do a good job," which needs a consistent coding scheme. If you plan to code open-ends, this is the time to do it. Even with CATI you may need to code open-ends. Each line of data has a "subject number," a unique ID for each interview or person who participated in the study. Then, each questionnaire is examined for errors or ambiguities.

For example, some people write media time estimates as "10 to 15 minutes."

You must decide what number to enter. In this case, average and standard rounding solves the problem (12.5 minutes rounds to 13 minutes, and "13" is entered into the spreadsheet).

You'll need consistent schemes for dealing with these issues. Having these rules available before interviewing saves a lot of time, but some ambiguities cannot be anticipated. Other problems are more difficult. If someone writes "all day" for a question asking about time watching television, does that mean 24 hours? Or 12 hours? Or will you just leave it blank or uncodable?

Before data entry you will need to name each variable. You'll need variable names even if you have direct computer entry during interviews. Most statistical analysis programs require variable names, and some require short names. Each scale or index item is treated as a different variable even though you will later compute a scale score. The items are added together in your spreadsheet or a total score is created in the data analysis. Table 22.1 contains an example of variable names for a data set using single variables and a scale composed of four items; the four items will be added together later in a new column in the spreadsheet.

The "meaning of codes" is used for the entries into the computer data file. If there are responses outside the appropriate range they are called "blanks" and no number is entered. Blanks can occur for many reasons: refusal to answer that question, an uncodable response or a question that only part of the sample answers. In this data set, if respondents refused to answer or didn't know an answer, then they were coded "blank."

CLEANING DATA

You will need to "clean" the spreadsheet or data file. This means to clean out bad data, verify that all of the entries match what respondents said and that responses are "in range." For example, if there is a "4" for gender, then that is an error because there should be only "1 = male" or "2 = female."

There are a number of techniques for cleaning data. One is *sight verification* where the numbers are visually compared with the original questionnaire responses. This can be tedious and time-consuming and may not catch all of the errors.

A second method is *double redundancy,* whereby two people independently enter data and then the files are compared for discrepancies. A variety of file comparison tools exist. Many come with standard computer software, and others are available as free downloads from the Internet. Classic tools include "COMP" in Windows and "Compare Documents" in Word that can check for differences between files. These are most useful for qualitative verbatim entries but can be used

Table 22.1
LIST OF VARIABLES, VARIABLE NAMES AND CODES

Variable	Variable Name	Meaning of Codes
ID number	ID	Unique ID, 001 thru 325
Newspaper reading, previous day	MINPAP	Number = minutes
TV viewing, previous day	HRSTV	Number = hours
Four-item "Need for Innovation Scale":		Responses: Strongly agree, Agree, Neutral, Disagree, Strongly disagree
Item one: I am willing to learn new ideas.	LRNNEW	5 = Strongly agree, 4 = Agree, 3 = Neutral, 2 = Disagree, 1 = Strongly disagree
Item two: I don't like to take a risk.	TAKERISK	1 = Strongly agree, 2 = Agree, 3 = Neutral, 4 = Disagree, 5 = Strongly disagree
Item three: I like to keep up with new technologies.	KEEPUP	5 = Strongly agree, 4 = Agree, 3 = Neutral, 2 = Disagree, 1 = Strongly disagree
Item four: I don't like to explore new technologies.	EXPLORE	1 = Strongly agree, 2 = Agree, 3 = Neutral, 4 = Disagree, 5 = Strongly disagree
Education	EDUC	1 = Less than high school degree 2 = High school degree 3 = Some college 4 = Bachelor's degree 5 = Graduate work +
Age	AGE	Number = Age in years
Gender	SEX	1 = Male, 2 = Female
"Need for innovation" scale score	INNOVATE	Sum of LRNNEW, TAKERISK, KEEPUP, EXPLORE Range: 4 to 20 Higher numbers = more likely to be an innovator
		Other answers = blank

for text from a spreadsheet. However, more direct methods for spreadsheets include custom file comparison tools like "Compare Suite" and "Excel Compare." In most of these tools one file is compared to the other file and any differences are noted in a third file which records "true" if the entries are the same and "false" if they are

Table 22.2
UNCLEANED DATA

ID	MINPAP	HRSTV	INET	HRSNET	EDUC	AGE	INCOME	SEX
1	90	7	2	0	5	81	4	1
2	38	4	2		3	83	2	2
3	5	4	1	1	4	41	4	1
4	18	15	1	1	4	32	4	1
5	30	1	1	1	4	70	2	1
6	30	2						
7	60	0	1	0	3	73	1	2
8	0	0	1	1	3	18	2	1
9	0	3	1	1	3	25	2	2
10	20	7	1	1	3	38	2	1
11	30	3	1	1	4	84	4	2
12	0	5	2		1	45	1	2
13	23	2	1	2	4	53	4	1
14	5	2	1	1	2	47	4	2
15	15	4						
16	13	0	1	0	4	22	2	2
17	20	0	1	1	5	63	4	2
18	0	3	1	0	4	35	3	2
19	20	1	1	0	5	39	4	2

not.

Even if two documents match there can be coding errors because of misinterpretations, original incorrect entries on the questionnaire or simple chance. Searching for "out of range" entries will catch other errors. For example, if only adults were interviewed and an age entry is "16," then you know to check the original questionnaire for the correct answer. COUNT, COUNTIF, IF and other spreadsheet functions can be helpful, or you can run a "frequencies" analysis, which lists the number of responses for each code. If codes appear that should not be there (e.g., a "6" for Gender), then you go back to the original questionnaire and enter the correct number. IF functions also work to make sure that follow-up questions match the filter question. For example, if you have "2" ("NO") to "Do you have access to the Internet?" you want to make sure there are no entries for other Internet use questions.

Table 22.2 shows part of the data from an Internet use mail-based survey after the first entry of data. Sight verification shows several errors. INET indicates whether a respondent has access to the Internet, and HRSNET shows how many hours they used the Internet on the precious day. For ID #1 there is no access to the Internet (code = 2) yet there is an entry for HRSNET (code = 0) when it should be blank. To check this requires going back to the paper questionnaire and finding out if INET should have been a "1" or if the "0" for HRSNET should not be there.

Also note the blanks for IDs 6 and 15. Perhaps the respondents returned a partially completed questionnaire or maybe the data entry people made an error. Again, checking the original questionnaires will verify the entries.

A CATI system should not allow the interviewer to enter out of range data. That is, if the interviewer hit "3" instead of "1" or "2" for yes/no, then the computer should prompt for a correct entry. However, there can be other errors, especially when coding open-ends.

CREATING NEW VARIABLES

The data set in Table 22.3 matches the list of variables, names and codes in Table 22.1. The data in Table 22.3 have been cleaned and are ready for analysis.

Once data have been cleaned you can create new variables. Remember that items for the scale were entered as separate variables. You simply add those items together and create the scale score. In the spreadsheet you can create a new column with the SUM function adding together the items for each row. In statistical software it is easy to create a scale score by using COMPUTE and other functions. For example, in Table 22.3, the Need for Innovation Scale (INNOVATE) has been created by adding together the four items LRNEW, TAKERISK, KEEPUP and EXPLORE.

It is also possible to do some basic analysis within the spreadsheet without resorting to complicated statistical analysis software. For example, AVERAGE, COUNT, CROSSTAB and other functions are useful. At the bottom of Table 22.4 the spreadsheet calculated the percentage of males and averages for MINPAP and HRSTV.

However, to get more complete or complex analyses statistical programs are better. Those programs can also produce tables, graphs and reports. The most popular are Statistical Package for the Social Sciences (SPSS) and Statistical Analysis System (SAS). Each of these has a Web site with an explanation of their functions and costs.

Table 22.3
CLEANED DATA FILE

ID	MINPAP	HRSTV	LRNNEW	TAKERISK	KEEPUP	EXPLORE	EDUC	AGE	SEX	INNOVATE
1	30	2	5	4	5	5	5	63	1	19
2	30	0	4	4	2	4	4	30	2	14
3	30	0	5	4	4	4	5	57	2	17
4	10	2	5	4	5	4	5	24	2	18
5	20	2	5	5	5	5	3	47	1	20
6	0	0	5	5	5	5	5	44	1	20
7	20	1	4	4	4	4	5	42	1	16
8	60	1	4	4	4	4	4	55	1	16
9	0	0	4	4	2	4	3	55	2	14
10	30	0	5	5	5	5	5	47	1	20
11	15	1	5	4	4	4	5	34	1	17
12	20	0	4	4	4	4	5	59	1	16
13	0	2	5	4	4	4	5	29	2	17
14	0	1	4	4	4	4	4	47	2	16
15	30	4	5	4	5	5	5	29	1	19
16	30	1	4	4	4	4	5	62	1	16
17	15	0	4	3	4	4	5	42	1	15
18	60	2	5	4	4	4	2	60	2	17
19	15	2	4	4	4	4	3	61	2	16
20	30	1	4	4	4	4	5	64	1	16
21	30	2	4	4	4	4	3	44	1	16
22	10	0	5	4	4	4	5	38	1	17
23	0	1	5	4	4	4	5	40	1	17
24	30	3	5	4	4	4	3	50	2	17
25	15	2	4	4	4	4	3	31	2	16
26	30	3	4	4	4	4	5	62	1	16
27	90	1	4	4	4	4	3	41	2	16
28	0	0	5	5	4	4	5	41	1	18
29	10	1	5	5	5	5	4	49	2	20

Table 22.4
DATA FILE

ID	MINPAP	HRSTV	LRNNEW	TAKERISK	KEEPUP	EXPLORE	EDUC	AGE	SEX	INNOVATE
1	30	2	5	4	5	5	5	63	1	19
2	30	0	4	4	2	4	4	30	2	14
3	30	0	5	4	4	4	5	57	2	17
4	10	2	5	4	5	4	5	24	2	18
5	20	2	5	5	5	5	3	47	1	20
6	0	0	5	5	5	5	5	44	1	20
7	20	1	4	4	4	4	5	42	1	16
8	60	1	4	4	4	4	4	55	1	16
9	0	0	4	4	2	4	3	55	2	14
10	30	0	5	5	5	5	5	47	1	20
11	15	1	5	4	4	4	5	34	1	17
12	20	0	4	4	4	4	5	59	1	16
13	0	2	5	4	4	4	5	29	2	17
14	0	1	4	4	4	4	4	47	2	16
15	30	4	5	4	5	5	5	29	1	19
16	30	1	4	4	4	4	5	62	1	16
17	15	0	4	3	4	4	5	42	1	15
18	60	2	5	4	4	4	2	60	2	17
19	15	2	4	4	4	4	3	61	2	16
20	30	1	4	4	4	4	5	64	1	16
21	30	2	4	4	4	4	3	44	1	16
22	10	0	5	4	4	4	5	38	1	17
23	0	1	5	4	4	4	5	40	1	17
24	30	3	5	4	4	4	3	50	2	17
25	15	2	4	4	4	4	3	31	2	16
26	30	3	4	4	4	4	5	62	1	16
27	90	1	4	4	4	4	3	41	2	16
28	0	0	5	5	4	4	5	41	1	18
29	10	1	5	5	5	5	4	49	2	20
							Percent Male		58.6	
Avg	22.8	1.2								

CHAPTER 23

BASIC ANALYSIS

A fter the data have been cleaned, it is time to do some basic analysis. This consists of three types: (1) descriptions of the sample, if used; (2) descriptive analysis; and (3) relational analysis (see "Descriptive vs. Relational Research" in Chapter 6).

Descriptive analysis is comprised of traditional single-variable descriptors, which include the percentage, mean, median and mode. Relational analysis can be very complicated, but two-variable analyses are fairly easy to understand and apply when using crosstabulation, mean comparison and correlation. The type of analysis employed depends upon the level of analysis of the variable or variables (see "Traditional Levels of Measurement" in Chapter 7).

DESCRIPTIONS OF THE SAMPLE

In Chapter 20, we calculated sampling error to determine the accuracy of a sample estimate under the assumption the sample was representative of the population. That assumption was based on having drawn a random sample. However, it is still possible to draw a sample that is not representative. This can happen by chance or because of other problems, like too many refusals. So other examinations of the sample are used to verify that the sample matches the population.

Outcome rates are statistics that helps determine whether a sample is usable. There are various types of rates that can be computed: completion rate, response rate, refusal rate and contact rate. These can be used in comparison with other studies of that population to determine the relative representativeness of the sample.

Suppose you know that mail studies tend to get low cooperation rates, around 35 percent for your population. Let's say that you only got 12 percent of a sample of addresses to respond. You might say it is so low that the sample cannot be representative of the population. Suppose, instead, you did telephone interviews and got a 47 percent cooperation rate. That's better than mail, but it still might not be good by comparison because other telephone studies obtain 65 percent or 70 percent in the market you are studying.

Calculating outcome rates can take several forms depending on your interest. The American Association for Public Opinion Research (AAPOR) recognizes four:

- *Response rate:* number of completed interviews divided by the number of eligible units in the sample.
- *Cooperation rate*: number of completed interviews divided by the number of eligible contacts.
- *Refusal rate*: number of refused interviews divided by the number of eligible contacts.
- *Contact rate*: number of units reached (whether they cooperated or not) divided by the total number of units in the sample.

AAPOR has formulas and definitions for each element that go into great detail, but the most important issue you must face is what comprises a completed interview. Obviously, someone answering all questions is a "complete," but you will have to determine what constitutes a usable response when only some of the questions have been answered ("partial complete").

The equation below uses the most typical formula for response rate (RR). It consists of the total completed interviews (I), which is completed plus partial completes that have been deemed usable. This is divided by all eligible contacts, which is completed (I) plus refused (R) plus noncontacts (NC). Refused includes totally refused plus partial completes that are not used in the analysis. Noncontacts include "no one answered," "answering machine, "voice mail" and other contacts where an interview was not completed. The calculation does not include noneligible attempts to contact, such as businesses if your sample is of residences. If you visit the AAPOR Web page, you can use a downloadable spreadsheet containing a response rate calculator.

$$RR = \frac{I}{I+R+NC}$$

Table 23.1
RESPONSE RATE DATA AND CALCULATION

	Eligible	Subtotal	Total
Completed interviews (I)	Completed all	312	354
	Partial interviews, usable	42	
Refusals (R)	Hang up, verbal refusal	68	101
	Partial complete, not usable	33	
Noncontacts (NC)	No answer, not at home	28	74
	Answering machine, voice mail, call block, etc., no completed interview	46	
	Not eligible		
	Businesses	22	29
	Government offices	3	
	Other: family moved, etc.	4	
Response rate calculation	$RR = \dfrac{354}{354 + 101 + 74}$ $RR = .669 = 66.9\%$		

The example in Table 23.1 is for a typical RDD telephone survey. You would use a similar method for mail, personal or electronic techniques. For example, instead of answering machine noncontacts, you would have a category "e-mail and received acknowledgment, but no returned questionnaire."

Insert the total eligible numbers into the formula — I is 354, R is 101, and NC is 74. Do not use the "not eligible" numbers. The RR is 66.9 percent.

Whether this rate is acceptable depends partly upon your expectations. For example, if other researchers are getting RRs of 54 percent, then your rate would be very good. But if others are consistently getting 75 percent or more, then you

Table 23.2
COMPARISON OF SOME DEMOGRAPHICS, SAMPLE VS. CENSUS

	Sample	Census
Males	45.1%	49.3%
Income		
$0-$19,999	23.2%	21.0%
$20,000-$39,999	20.4%	22.9%
$40,000 and over	56.4%	56.1%
Home ownership rate	44.1%	48.4%
Race		
White	72.2%	70.1%
African-American	1.3%	8.1%
Asian	14.2%	13.1%
Other	12.3%	8.7%
Median age (years)	38.2	35.4

might raise questions about your procedures that needs to be fixed. (That doesn't mean your research is useless, because you can determine how well your sample matches some variables in the population, as explained in the next section.)

Assessing representativeness is done even if your response rate is acceptable. You still can have a "bum" sample just by chance (remember from the normal curve that only 95 percent of the samples are close to the true population value). So check to see if your sample matches the population. Usually, sample demographics are compared to population demographics and other known characteristics, and if they are close you are more confident that you got a representative sample.

Demographics are compared in Table 23.2. If you had N = 300, most of the comparisons are within sampling error. For example, gender is OK because the 4.2 percent difference between the sample and the population is less than the sampling error of ±5.6 percent. However, African Americans are *under-represented* because the 6.8 percent difference is greater than the ±1.3 percent sampling error. This does not mean you throw out the study. You can still use the sample because most comparisons are close.

To address the under-representativeness you could (1) note the areas of under-representation and urge caution in interpreting results that use those variables, (2) use a weighting procedure to deal with the under-represented variables or (3)

JOEY REAGAN

conduct relational analyses to see if those who are under-represented responded differently that others (i.e., compare African-American results with the other races' results).

WEIGHTING

What if your sample is different than the population? Suppose your sample has 67 percent women. You can still use the sample if you "balance" the sample; that is, give more "weight" to men's responses and less to women's. Since women make up twice the proportion of the sample than men, you would "double" each response for men. Weighting assumes that the people who were not in the sample are similar to the people who are. Weighting is usually carried out by a statistical analysis program.

Be careful of samples using a lot of weighting because they can give unreliable results. For example, if most active people are not at home when called, then weighting exaggerates the opinions of the small number of active people who are at home, and if these people are different from those who are not at home, then the sample will not be representative of that group. The assumption is that the under-represented group is representative of the group from which they come.

Before weighting, it is advisable to compare the groups. For example, compare men and women for all variables in the study. If there's very little difference, then weighting is not an issue.

Prior to conducting a study, if you expect the final sample will over-represent a group, try to balance during data collection. In the United States, women are about twice as likely to answer the phone than men. Instead of waiting until the data are collected, alternately ask to interview a male in the household and then a female.

One additional problem with weighting is that it makes interpreting statistical tests of significance more difficult. Generally speaking, unless there is a significant problem with representation in your sample, you need not weight the data.

DESCRIPTIVE ANALYSIS

Descriptive analysis is a single-variable analysis. Although you may have many variables in a study, you analyze one variable at a time. For each nominal or ordinal variable, you want the percentages in each category. For each interval or ratio variable, you want the means. Statisticians also compute other statistics like "standard deviation," "variance" and "skew," but I have not included these here.

Table 23.3
IMPORTANCE OF FACTORS IN SELECTING A HOSPITAL
(Used by permission of Kadlec Medical Center)

	Average Importance (1-10)
Local, community oriented	7.7
Convenient location	8.0
Reputation	8.8
Your doctor's recommendation	8.5
Modern equipment	9.1
Qualified physicians	9.6

These concepts relate to the idea of "distribution," which is covered toward the end of this chapter.

Descriptive analyses can do two things. First, they can give you an overall feel for the population, such as what percentage own homes or what average is spent on entertainment each year per household. Second, these analyses can answer specific research questions, such as the one illustrated in Table 23.3, where Kadlec Medical Center asked about how important certain factors were in selecting a hospital. Although each is analyzed separately (each factor is a variable), the six variables are all in one table. Each is measured with a "direct magnitude estimate" (one to ten, with ten being "very important"), which is an interval level of measurement.

Descriptive analyses can be very simple and are sometimes presented as a narrative in the report rather than a table. The example below is from a report on people's knowledge about King County (Washington) Camp Fire.

Of the 144 nonmember adults who participated in the survey:

- ► 95 percent said they recognized the name "Camp Fire" and could correctly describe it as a youth organization.
- ► 65 percent said friends and relatives are a source of information about youth organizations.

Descriptive analyses consist of *frequencies* (the number of responses for each

Table 23.4

BASIC ANALYSIS FOR EACH LEVEL OF MEASUREMENT

Level of Measurement	Example	Analysis
Nominal	Race	Frequencies Percentages Mode
Ordinal	Income, in categories	Frequencies Percentages Median Mode
Interval	Scale score	All of above + Mean
Ratio	Age, in years	All of above + Mean

category), *percentages* in each category, the *mean* (or average), the *median* (the score that separates the responses into equal halves) and the *mode* (the category or value with the most responses). Table 23.4 shows the appropriate analysis based on each level of measurement.

- For nominal level data, you can calculate frequencies and percentages in each category, and the mode. You can't use median because there is no rank order to the categories.
- For ordinal level you can calculate frequencies and percentages in each category plus the median and the mode. But, since the categories for nominal and ordinal are not "real" numbers, you cannot calculate an average.
- For interval level you can use all analyses.
- For ratio level you can use all analyses.

In a simplified spreadsheet Table 23.5 shows twenty subjects with an ID and responses for two variables, one with real numbers — MINPAP, minutes reading a newspaper on the previous day — and one categorical — INCOME, annual household income in categories (1= $0-$15,000; 2= $15,001-$25,000; 3= $25,001-$35,000; 4= $35,001-$45,000; 5= over $45,000).

You can see that the descriptive results for MINPAP are a mean of 20.75, a

Table 23.5
BASIC ANALYSIS FOR TIME WITH NEWSPAPER AND INCOME

ID	MINPAP	INCOME
1	30	3
2	30	2
3	30	3
4	10	4
5	20	1
6	0	2
7	20	2
8	60	3
9	0	2
10	30	5
11	15	3
12	20	5
13	0	2
14	0	3
15	0	3
16	30	4
17	30	3
18	15	2
19	60	4
20	15	1
Mean	20.75	
Median	20	3
Mode	30	3

median of 20, and a mode of 30. For INCOME the mean is not appropriate because it is an ordinal variable, but the median is 3 and the mode is also 3.

Tables often contain frequencies, designated *f*. They are usually reported along with percentages. Table 23.6 shows both the frequencies and percentages for "income" in categories.

RELATIONAL ANALYSIS

Relational analysis compares two or more variables. For example, if you want to know if males are different than females in their attitudes, compare gender with attitude. Or, if you want to know if purchase behavior is different for active vs. inactive people, compare purchase behavior with activity. I will cover only relations

Table 23.6
DESCRIPTIVE RESULTS FOR INCOME, FREQUENCIES AND PERCENTAGES

	f	%
$0-$14,999	54	14.7
$15,000-$24,999	78	21.3
$25,000-$34,999	101	27.5
$35,000-$44,999	71	19.3
$45,000 and above	63	17.2
N	367	100.0

between two variables, but there are analyses and tables for three or more variables (some of which are covered in Chapter 25). Relational tables are more complicated than descriptive tables, because they combine different levels of measurement, and each requires a different analysis. The most used analyses are shown in Table 23.7 and are discussed below.

CROSSTABULATION

If you had two categorical (nominal or ordinal) variables you would use crosstabulation, as in the example in Table 23.8 where a campaign is

Table 23.7
RELATIONAL ANALYSIS FOR COMBINATION OF LEVELS OF MEASUREMENT

Variable 1 Level of Measurement	Variable 2 Level of Measurement	Example	Analysis
Nominal OR Ordinal	Nominal OR Ordinal	V1: Gender V2: Race	Crosstabulation
Nominal OR Ordinal	Interval OR Ratio	V1: Gender V2: Hrs. TV, previous day	Means by Subgroups
Interval OR Ratio	Interval OR Ratio	V1: Annual income, in $ V2: Image scale score	Correlation

Table 23.8
PERCEPTION OF NEWSLETTER TRUTHFULNESS, BEFORE VS. AFTER CAMPAIGN

	Before	After
The information I receive in the company newsletter is truthful	%	%
Agree	24	54
Disagree	71	38
Other	5	8

evaluated by relating perceptions of truthfulness with time period in the campaign ("time" can be a variable).

MEANS BY SUBGROUPS

If one categorical variable (nominal or ordinal) and one real number variable (interval or ratio) are used, then you apply means by subgroups, simply comparing the mean of one group with another. Table 23.9 shows the relation between scale score for image of the company and gender.

CORRELATION

Correlation is neither a percentage nor an average. It is a special statistic whose number is between "–1" and "+1" (including "0"). A "–1" is a *perfect negative relationship*; "+1" is a *perfect positive relationship*; and "0" is no relationship at all. Research results almost never get exactly "0," "1," or "–1." Correlation is used when both variables are "real" numbers (interval or ratio). Correlation is usually designated with an "r."

A positive correlation, like ".54" or ".11," means that as the values of

Table 23.9
PERCEPTION OF COMPANY IMAGE, MALES VS. FEMALES

	Males	Females
Mean Image Scale Score	54.8	44.2

Table 23.10
CORRELATION OF IMAGE WITH THREE VARIABLES

	Correlation
Image and Salary	.38
Image and Length of Employment	−.66
Image and Number of Friends	.03

one variable increase, so do the values of another. In Table 23.10, as salary goes up, so does the image score (.38 in the example).

A *negative correlation* like "−.13" or "−.64" means that as the values of one variable increase, the values of another decrease. Table 23.10 shows a negative correlation between image and length of employment. As number of years of employment increases, the image score goes down (−.66).

Zero correlation (no relation) means that as the values of one variable increase, the values of another stay the same or change randomly. In the table, as the number of friends goes up, image stays the same (.03 is close to 0.00).

In addition to telling whether a relation is positive or negative, you can tell how strong a relationship is and if one relation is stronger than another. Looking at the three correlations above, "−.66" is the strongest because it has the highest absolute value, and ".03" is the weakest.

Most industry quantitative research reports contain percentages and means exclusively. That's because most people who use those numbers are familiar with simple percentages and averages but not correlation. However, when dealing with relational analyses, crosstabulations or means usually are insufficient with interval and ratio variables.

DISTRIBUTION

Distribution shows how the responses vary among the values. Distribution is obvious when you use percentages because you get a percentage or frequency for each category. However, when you examine means you don't know anything about how much the responses varied until you look at the distribution. Table 23.11 shows distributions of the number of times per month that employees read the in-house newsletter. All distributions have the same mean, but the distributions are different

Table 23.11
EXAMPLE OF SAME MEANS WITH DIFFERENT DISTRIBUTIONS

	Distribution 1	Distribution 2	Distribution 3
0 times	3%	12%	30%
1 time	5%	12%	15%
2 times	7%	13%	3%
3 times	35%	13%	2%
4 times	35%	13%	2%
5 times	7%	13%	3%
6 times	5%	12%	15%
7 times	3%	12%	30%
Mean	3.5 days	3.5 days	3.5 days

and may lead to different interpretations.

In the first distribution, the mean is a good representation of what most employees do, but the mean would be misleading for the other distributions. In distribution two, the responses are equally scattered, but in distribution three some employees read a lot and some read very little — most employees are at the extremes.

Thus, strategies to get employees to read would be different depending on the distribution. For example, the first would imply just trying to raise the average, getting almost all to read more often, while distribution three implies targeting those who read very little.

DEALING WITH VERBATIMS/OPEN-END RESPONSES

A problem with open-ended responses is that they are often difficult to interpret. Table 23.12 is taken from the survey question, "What is your general impression of Kadlec Medical Center?" You can see the range of responses. Some comments are clearly positive ("helpful," "competent"); others are clearly negative ("overpriced"); but some are difficult to interpret. What does "suck" mean beyond being negative? Is "a corporation" positive or negative?

You must refrain from focusing too much on specific comments. Sometimes one respondent will make an extreme comment, like "billing blood suckers," that

Table 23.12
LIST OF VERBATIMS
(Used by permission of Kadlec Medical Center)

Good (22 mentions)	Efficient (4)	Long wait at ER
Pretty good (14)	Too slow (5)	Busy place
Professional (9)	Improved (2)	Billing blood suckers
Fine (9)	Better than others (2)	Snobbish
OK/fair (6)	Cold people	Helpful
Excellent (6)	Suck	Competent
Favorable (5)	Advanced technology	Overpriced
Modern (5)	A corporation	As reputable as others
Like it (5)	Bright and cheery	Rapacious
Clean (4)	E.R. pitiful	

can elicit a gut reaction, "Oh, my god, we need to fix that," even though it represents less than one-half percent of the sample.

Still, single comments can alert you to potential problems. The comment "long wait at ER" was only mentioned by one person, but the sample might have contained only twenty people who had been to Kadlec's emergency room. An internal investigation of the ER might show that there are indeed long waits, and it might be easy to keep patients informed of the wait time. Or you can make sure to probe more about the issue in the next market survey.

Numeric codes can be generated for words and comments if you can define categories. When you want to generate categories for questions — like "How do you feel about XYZ Company," or "What do you think are the important health issues in our community?" — you must go through a formal *coding session.* That involves assigning two or more people to examine all responses and form some agreement on the categories along with a determination about which response goes into which category.

The coders independently rate each message on criteria you have predetermined: positive or negative, strength of response, and so on. Then their coding is compared. If they agree, then their codes are accepted. If they do not agree, then they may discuss the issue and reach a consensus. You will never get 100 percent agreement, so for large data sets it is important to compute *intercoder reliability,* which is a measure of agreement. There are several different intercoder reliability statistics. You can download free software from the Internet that calculates "percent agreement," "alpha," "reliability," "rho," and other estimates.

CHAPTER 24

SIGNIFICANCE TESTS AND EXPLAINED VARIANCE

T ables with numbers do not tell you how accurate those numbers are. Remember sampling error? It's possible those numbers are just chance occurrences, or the relations you think you found don't really exist in the population. In addition, each study can generate tens to hundreds of possible relations. How do you know which relations are the strongest or most important?

You deal with these issues by doing *significance tests* and estimates of *explained variance*. The purpose of this chapter is to introduce you to these tests and estimates, not make you a statistician. Your consultant or research director should be able to provide the necessary tests.

SIGNIFICANCE

Significance has a special meaning among statisticians. At its basic level, significance is a statement about the probability of what appears to be a relation between two variables. We can only estimate that probability if we use random samples. Significance should not be used with nonrandom samples.

Conventionally, significance is expressed as the probability that the results are just chance variations rather than a "true" relation. That probability should be as low as possible. In other words, you should take only a small chance that a relation does not exist in the population. As a rule of thumb, social science uses

Table 24.1
COMMON SIGNIFICANCE TESTS FOR VARIOUS LEVELS OF MEASUREMENT

Levels of Measurement	Analysis	Significance Test
Both nominal or ordinal	Crosstabulation (percent)	χ^2
One nominal or ordinal, One interval or ratio	Means by subgroups (averages for each category)	t-test
Both interval or ratio	Correlation (r)	t-test for Pearson's r

"p<.05," which means there is less than a 5 percent chance that your sample results are accidental occurrences. In other words, you have a 95 percent probability that the relation really exists. When social scientists say, "Our results are significant," that's what they mean.

Significance tests are used to figure out that "p" number. There are literally hundreds of significance tests. The ones used most often are those for crosstabulations, subgroup means and correlation. Most tests are calculated by statistical programs like Statistical Package for the Social Sciences (SPSS) and Statistical Analysis System (SAS). Each of the tests in Table 24.1 can be found in a statistical program and will produce a probability for each relation you want to test.

If one of the above tests produces a probability of p<.05, then you have most likely found a relation. You can say this in many ways:

- "The relation is significant."
- "The results are not just chance results."
- "The results are different than those expected by chance."
- "There is a high probability that the relation exists in the population."

EXAMPLES OF SIGNIFICANCE TESTS

If your research question asks about a difference and you found no difference, then do not proceed to a significance test. If you hypothesized that one group would be higher than another and the opposite is your result, then proceed no farther. Only if your results come out like you predicted should you continue. The following examples are taken from a survey about technology adoption.

Chi-square (χ^2) is the test for two nominal or ordinal level variables. In Table 24.2 you will see percentages for each "crossing" of categories. These are called

Table 24.2

COMPARISON OF MALE VS. FEMALE INTERNET ACCESS

Have Internet access?	Males	Females
	Gender	
	%	%
Yes	74.2	71.3
No	25.9	28.7
n	89	157
$\chi^2 = 0.179$		
p = .672		

"cells," and they consist of: (1) male-have access, (2) male-do-not-have access, (3) female-have access and (4) female-do-not. The "n" is the size of each subsample. Once the χ^2 is calculated it is compared to a table of probabilities for χ^2 (available online or in many statistics books), which shows the probabilities associated with each value. Statistical software is easier and will output the probabilities.

Suppose, based on "diffusion of innovations theory," you had a hypothesis: "Males are more likely than females to have access to the Internet." You would compare what percentage of males had access to what percentage of females had access. In the table you see that males are slightly more likely to have Internet access (74.1 percent vs. 71.3 percent), but the relation is not significant because the probability is .672, which is *greater than* .05. So rather than having a "significant" result you would say,

- "The relation is not significant."
- "The results are just chance results."
- "The results are not different from those expected by chance."
- "There is a low probability that the relation exists in the population."

The *t-test for difference of means* is used to compare means from two subgroups. So one variable has two categories and the other is interval or ratio. In this case, your statistical software calculates a "*t*-value" and also the probability associated with that value. Based upon conflicting previous research, suppose you had a research question that asked, "Do people who have access to the Internet own

Table 24.3
COMPARISON OF TECHNOLOGIES OWNED WITH INTERNET ACCESS

	Have Internet access?	
	Yes	No
Mean number of technologies owned:	7.8	4.9
n	178	68
	$t = 8.49$; $p<.000001$	

more or fewer technologies than those who do not have access?" Notice that this is a question that only asks if they are different, not predicting that one group is higher than the other.

In Table 24.3 you see that those with access own more technologies than those without (7.8 vs. 4.9). That seems like a big difference, but you must look at the significance test to see if that is a chance difference. In this case the test shows a probability vastly lower than $p<.05$. So you can say, "This is a significant result" or "The difference in the averages probably exists in the population from which the sample was chosen."

The *t-test for a correlation* is used when you have two "real" number variables (interval or ratio). Suppose previous research has shown that younger people are more likely to adopt technologies. So you hypothesize: "Younger people own more technologies than older people." You expect that as age increases, the number of technologies owned decreases. So you predict a negative relationship.

Table 24.4 shows that the relation is indeed negative, and the probability is lower than .05; thus, you can confidently say, "The relation is significant" and "Younger people own more technologies than older people."

You can't use a *t*-test for three or more categories. It is for two categories or groups only. You use an *F-test for multiple means* for three or more categories in one variable and interval or ratio in the other. You might compare five racial subgroups or you might conduct an experiment that has three or more treatments. If you were interested in knowing the impact of ad placement on whether Internet users clicked on an ad, you might ask — "Does the number of click-throughs vary based on ad placement?" — and then create an experiment where you tested whether the IV (ad placement) caused changes in the DV (number of click-

Table 24.4
CORRELATION OF NUMBER OF TECHNOLOGIES OWNED WITH AGE

	Correlation
	$-.414$
N	241
	$t = -8.36$; $p < .000001$

throughs).

Table 24.5 shows the results for an experiment that tested the impact of various layouts for Web page ads on click-throughs for those ads. Four layouts (categories) are compared: (1) ads on top, (2) ads in the right column, (3) ads in a left column and (4) ads embedded in the center within the text. It looks like embedded ads have the most click-throughs followed by ads on top, ads in left column and ads in right column. However, the F-test shows a nonsignificant relation. In other words the differences could be by chance, so you cannot conclude that various treatments in your experiment caused differences in clicking on ads. You would say:

- "The relation is not significant."
- "The results are just chance results."
- "The results are not different from those expected by chance."
- "There is a low probability that the relation exists in the population."
- "There is a low probability that ad placement causes click-throughs."
- "There is not a cause-and-effect in this experiment."

OTHER CONSIDERATIONS IN SIGNIFICANCE TESTING

For the sake of simplicity and ease of understanding, I have not included other considerations that statisticians make. For example, when you hypothesize a "direction," such as one group being greater than another, you are using *a one-tail probability*, whereas when you just ask if groups are different then you use a *two-tail probability*. Most tests also use "degrees of freedom," a measure of how many groups or values a respondent can move among.

Table 24.5
AD PLACEMENT IMPACT ON CLICK-THROUGHS

	Experimental Treatment			
	Ads on top	Ads in right Column	Ads in left Column	Ads Embedded in text
Mean click-throughs	8.45	5.72	7.24	9.79
n	56	56	56	56
	$F = 2.079; p = 0.104$			

There are many other significance tests not covered here: single-sample t-test, matched-pairs t-test, sign test, Cochran's Q, and so on. They depend on the level of measurement and how the samples are drawn. What's important is that you understand what significance tests are and why they are used. Your consultant or research director should be able to select the most appropriate test.

A NOTE ON GENERALIZABILITY

Remember the concept *generalizability* in Chapter 8? Keep in mind that you only do significance tests to generalize to or to make inferences to a population if you use a random sample. These tests are not appropriate for convenience, volunteer or other nonrandom samples. In addition, you can only generalize to the population from which the sample was drawn. So the results cannot be applied to another locale, group or any other target.

A NOTE ON USING A CENSUS

If you do a census then you are not using a sample, so significance tests are not appropriate. After all, you have exact numbers, not estimates, and a census, therefore, has zero sampling error, *ceteris paribas* ("all things being equal"). A census is more accurate than a survey.

EXPLAINED VARIANCE

Significance is often overemphasized. All it indicates is whether a relation exists. It does not tell you how important that relation is. With a large enough sample, almost any variable will be significantly related with any other variable. You would make a different decision about how to target your promotion if you found that gender was only 1 percent related to your image versus 25 percent related, especially if you had other variables that were more strongly related to image.

Explained variance allows you to determine the strengths of relations. It estimates how much of a change in one variable produces a magnitude of change in another. We usually express this strength as a percentage, such as "13 percent of the change in one variable is related to the change in another variable." This is also called the *effect size.*

These estimates range between zero and one (0 percent to 100 percent) with zero meaning there is no relationship, and 1.0 meaning there is a perfect relationship. Of course, we rarely get 1.0, but now we can compare the strengths of different correlations or other relation estimates. There are many estimates depending on the types of variables and analyses used. These include,

- C (Contingency coefficient), used for crosstabulation
- η^2 (eta^2), used for means by subgroups
- r^2, used for correlation
- R^2, used for some multivariate analyses

As usual, there are many more than these four explained variance estimates, and statistical analysis programs will generate the estimates. Take the four examples of significance in Tables 24.2 thorough 24.5. The appropriate estimates of explained variance are in Table 24.6.

You can see the strongest relation is for the correlation. The other three are weaker relations. If there is no relation or a small relation then explained variance will be close to zero. This is not surprising for the two nonsignificant relations (the crosstabulation and the means for the multi-group experiment). However, the means for the two-group comparison, the *t*-test, was "highly significant" in Table 24.3, yet the explained variance is pretty low at 3.4 percent.

Explained variance becomes more critical when you are trying to determine which of many variables has the largest impact on or relation with a dependent variable. Say you have three variables (gender, salary, length of employment) related to image of your company (scale score). Assuming gender is categorical, salary and length of employment are ratio, and the image scale is interval, you might

Table 24.6
EXPLAINED VARIANCE FOR FOUR EXAMPLES

Analysis	Explained Variance Estimate	Explained Variance Result
Crosstabulation	C	Table 24.2 C = 0.027 or 2.7%
Means by subgroups (for two categories)	η^2	Table 24.3 $\eta^2 = 0.034$ or 3.4%
Correlation	r^2	Table 24.4 $r^2 = 0.171$ or 17.1%
Means by subgroups (for three or more categories)	η^2	Table 24.5 $\eta^2 = 0.027$ or 2.7%

get the estimates in Table 24.7 where the relation to gender is the weakest.

The problem with doing several bivariate analyses is that they may not be "statistically independent." For example, you could compare males and females on Internet access, and then compare males and females on technologies owned, and then compare males and females on online purchase behavior; these are not independent because there are many interrelations between variables, such as Internet access affecting online purchase. The examples above, Tables 24.3 and 24.4, are not independent because age might affect Internet access and that relation

Table 24.7
COMPARING EXPLAINED VARIANCE FOR
THREE PREDICTORS OF COMPANY IMAGE

		p	Explained Variance
Gender: Male mean image score Female mean image score	37.5 30.2	.043	$\eta^2 = .049$ or 4.9%
Salary correlation with Image	.36	.002	$r^2 = 140$ or 14.0%
Length of employment correlation with Image	.13	.392	$r^2 = .017$ or 1.7%

has not been accounted for.

This makes sense. Human behavior is not caused by a single variable. Many variables — demographics, lifestyle, attitudes — combine to determine people's behavior. The best analysis is one that accounts for all variables at the same time: *multivariate analysis* which is covered in the next chapter.

A NOTE ON CAUSE-AND-EFFECT

Although your results indicate significant and strong relations, that still doesn't tell you there is cause-and-effect. However, it is a good start in the right direction. At this point, of the three elements of cause-and-effect, you may have satisfied two: by finding significance you have demonstrated a relation and by showing a strong relation you have some evidence toward eliminating other causes. If you had conducted the experiment, or if you logically demonstrate time order, as in gender preceding Internet use, then you have a stronger case for a cause.

CHAPTER 25

A BRIEF LOOK AT MULTIVARIATE ANALYSIS

So far you have been exposed to descriptive analysis, single-variable analysis and bivariate (two-variable) relational analysis. Surely you know the cost of a product is not the sole determinate of its purchase and the size of salary alone does not cause employee image of a company. Obviously, attitudes, behaviors and other variables are shaped by a multitude of factors, such as age, salary, length of employment, education, values, needs and lifestyle.

You could, of course, compare many variables with separate correlations. For example, you could do various significance tests of cost with product sales, then need with product sales, then size of economy with product sales, then seasonal cycle with product sales. But that would not be appropriate because each of those IVs is also related to each other variable. For example, size of the economy may affect overall sales in the long term even while cycles affect sales in the short term.

So there must be a way to analyze many variables at one time. There is, and it's called *multivariate analysis*. You can perform significance tests and estimate explained variance for all of the variables taken together or individual IVs. Moreover, you can tell which variables have the strongest relations.

This chapter only briefly summarizes some of the multivariate analyses. It does not attempt to teach you how to conduct them or the details of their statistics. However, you should note conceptual similarities to bivariate analyses such as significance and explained variance.

AN EXAMPLE OF MULTIVARIATE ANALYSIS

Producers of technologies want to know who is likely to purchase their merchandise, partly because this information will help them create advertising and promotional campaigns. They may ask, "What are the variables that determine how much people plan to spend on LCD televisions in the next six months?" The results in Table 25.1 are based on interval or ratio variables, dollars, hours, etc.

Since all variables are either interval or ratio level of measurement, and there is a single DV with multiple IVs, one possible analysis is *linear regression*. Regression produces a set of coefficients, just like plotting slopes in high school algebra. Standardized coefficients allow comparison across the IVs. If significant, you can compare the absolute value of the coefficients, and the larger ones have the larger relations. The sign of the coefficient tells you whether the relation is positive or negative.

There are two types of significance tests. The F-test is for an overall relation between all the IVs and the DV — in the example the overall relation is significant, $p<.05$. The t-tests are for relations between individual variables and the DV. In the example, only "age" and "income" are significantly related to the DV. The other variables are nonsignificant. You will also see "R^2," which is the measure of explained variance for the entire analysis.

To determine if your analysis is useful, you first need to look at the overall analysis. If it is not significant, you would say that none of the relationships would be useful in predicting LCD TV expenditure. However, in this example it is significant, but you also need to look at R^2 of .121. It explains 12.1 percent of the variance. Since it's not 100 percent, there are other variables that you haven't examined that may also be related to the DV. In fact, there are probably many or perhaps a few strong ones because so much of the variance is unexplained (100 percent $- R^2 = 87.9$ percent unexplained). You should analyze other variables in your study or include new variables in future studies.

Next look at individual variables to find the strongest relationships. There are only two significant individual relations — "age" and "income" — both positive relations, and income is stronger.

OTHER MULTIVARIATE ANALYSES

Most advanced analyses require some expertise, usually calling in help from a statistical consultant. The basics of these techniques are simple, but some of the

Table 25.1
RELATION OF EXPECTED EXPENDITURE ON LCD TELEVISION WITH DEMOGRAPHICS, TECHNOLOGY AND MEDIA USE VARIABLES

	Standardized Coefficient	Significance*
Independent variables	β	p
Hours TV, previous day	.061	.416
Hours Internet use, previous day	.080	.293
Income	.290	.001
Age of current TV	.108	.177
Minutes reading newspaper, previous day	−.161	.181
Age	.216	.049
Number of video technologies owned	.094	.376
Number of other technologies owned	−.107	.221

Overall p = .010**

R^2 = .121

*Based on t-test for one IV with DV

**Based on F-test for all IVs together with DV

statistical details are daunting. The techniques described below are only a handful of those available but are among those most used by social scientists.

Linear regression, as in the example above, uses several variables to predict a single DV. For instance, you may want to know the factors that are related to employee job satisfaction. These may include gender, age, salary, company function participation, length of employment, time reading company newsletter, job classification, perceived autonomy and attitude toward fellow employees. The results may give you several strategies to increase employee satisfaction.

Discriminant analysis is used when the DV is nominal or ordinal. Suppose you wanted to find the factors that relate to whether people subscribe to a cable television "on-demand" service. The subscription DV is nominal (do subscribe/do not subscribe), and many IVs can be used: income, DVD ownership, VCR ownership, etc.

Cluster analysis categorizes a population into homogeneous subgroups similar to how species are categorized (e.g., primates, mammals). Essentially it develops a taxonomy that collects similar people together on several characteristics or behaviors. A typical example is geographic clusters of postal codes whose residents have similar demographics, read similar magazines, have similar purchase behaviors and lead similar lifestyles. Such designations can lead to strategies about the best way to reach people with similar purchase behavior by more efficiently targeting the similar media they use or by using direct mail advertising.

Time-series analysis helps understand behavior that is affected by variables at different previous time periods. The analysis allows you to anticipate future behavior as these causative factors occur. For example, marketers know that brand awareness precedes purchase and can be used to predict future revenue. Another example is the study of the relation between electronic promotion and future revenue. At time one, an e-mail promotion with a link to a retail site is sent; at time two, recipients click through and explore the site and at time three a recipient places an order. This process can be tracked so that order volume can be anticipated and you can evaluate promotions of the site.

Mapping is one way to develop positioning strategies. It can discover your position in the minds of your target and can suggest strategies to overcome disparities. Maps can be derived from both qualitative and quantitative data. Qualitative mapping usually involves a large number of in-depth interviews. The research tries to find the interviewees' underlying thoughts about the product or organization, how they perceive their fit with the product or organization and how they react to different message strategies. A map like this might help understand consumer attitudes toward both the company and product and suggest areas that need attention.

Quantitative mapping tries to precisely measure differences between concepts about a product, service or entity. "Metric Multidimensional Scaling" (MMDS) is a quantitative mapping technique that can be used to draw a multidimensional map of concepts. For example, you can map how close or how far segments of your market are to your radio station along with how close they are to other related concepts like "country music," "current," "hard" and "pop."

Factor analysis is used to look for patterns among multiple variables, including items used in a scale. For example, you may have developed a scale to measure employee satisfaction, but it may have several "factors" or subsets, such as satisfaction with work, satisfaction with communication and satisfaction with colleagues. This technique can also help you determine the reliability of scale items.

If items do not relate to each other, then you would suspect there is something wrong with them.

Reliability is often used to assess the usefulness of scale and index items. An "alpha" (α) is computed, between zero and one, that shows how related the items are to each other. The higher the number, the more reliable the scale or index. Along with the α are "item-total correlations" that are similar to correlation except the relations are between an individual item and the scale score. If an item-total correlation is low, you would suspect there is something wrong with the item.

Conjoint analysis is similar to mapping, but tries to overcome the problems people have in identifying the importance of attributes. Most people would say, "All" when asked to pick out the important attributes for a product or service from a list. Conjoint analysis attempts to determine the trade-offs or relative values of the various attributes of a product or service. However, it attempts to measure and analyze the attributes together.

For example, cost, size, complexity, ease of shopping for a product and other attributes may be important, but they vary relative to each other. Questions usually relate to perceptions, such as "How likely...," "How much do you prefer...," "How important..." and so on. Numerical estimates are used, such as "0 percent to 100 percent likely." These numbers can then be entered into an "analysis of variance" to derive index numbers for each attribute that forecast the strength of each attribute in predicting purchase or use of a product or service.

CHAPTER 26

ESSENTIAL QUALITIES OF RESEARCH REPORTS

T his chapter is not meant to teach you how to write research reports, but rather, what to expect when you receive one. You will be reading many research reports and you will need to make reasoned judgments about the quality of the research. This includes whether the sampling technique was appropriate or whether the conclusions are generalizable to your population. The details of a report will allow you to:

- Provide information to help with your needs and goals
- Answer your RQs
- Replicate your study
- Compare your study to other studies that were done of the same population.
- Provide information about how the study was conducted when your clients or advertisers ask, "How do we know we can trust your study?"
- Draw your own conclusions and compare your conclusions to those of your consultant or research director.

This chapter focuses on professional reports, but academic reports are similar, although academicians emphasize previous research and methods much more.

Reports in scientific journals usually begin with an extensive review of previous research and detailed examination of the methods. They emphasize developing new measures, testing those measures, analyzing how well their methods test their hypotheses and verifying the reliability of their measures. Applied researchers also place importance on using reliable and valid techniques, but the obvious emphasis is on how the results can solve real-world problems.

ELEMENTS OF A REPORT

A full report should provide all the details of the study so a reader can judge the quality of the research and adequacy of the methods. The results in the report can be used to develop creative and other strategies. Most reports contain the following elements.

EXECUTIVE SUMMARY

This is a one- to two-page summary of the project. You, your staff and board of directors may not have time to read the entire report, so an executive summary is essential. It should include a brief description of the project, basic methodology of the study and summary of results. The focus should be on actionable results, such as, "These are the five things you can do to improve" or "These are the strengths of the competitors."

INTRODUCTION

Usually short, it provides a rationale for the study, including the needs statement, other related research and RQs.

METHOD (OR METHODOLOGY)

This section details how the study was conducted and usually includes a summary of the questions, stimuli, procedures, dates of the data collection, sampling error, representativeness and other details.

QUESTIONNAIRE (OR OTHER SCRIPTS, AGENDAS, ETC.).

These are necessary to understand how the data were collected as well as being useful for replications and other follow-up research. They are often in an appendix rather than the body of the report.

DESCRIPTION OF THE SAMPLE

If a sample is used, the frame, sampling technique and other details help evaluate whether the results are generalizable to the target population.

RESULTS

For quantitative studies, these are the numerical results that answer the research questions and are the main body of the report. For qualitative studies, these may include a moderator's or interviewer's interpretation or summary of what went on during the interviews, along with a documentation and interpretation of the comments, such as "Message 'A' resonated well in Detroit but not in Philadelphia," with illustrative comments.

SUMMARY

This should focus the reader on the most important or actionable results.

With the full report, you should get an exact copy of any data generated by the study. That includes a copy of the data file and lists of verbatims from a quantitative inquiry, or a copy of transcripts and video and audio recordings from a qualitative effort. This should include a codebook because your interpretation of the results won't be useful if you can't interpret the meaning of responses. In addition, you should have contact information from your consultant in case you have questions about the study or need additional analyses performed.

The styles and contents of reports vary depending on the writer, preferences of the users of the report and nature of the data. For example, some reports use pie charts, others use bar charts and some use only data tables with no charts.

You will not usually find a summary in a ratings report because the purpose is merely to provide data that can be used to estimate audience size for specific intentions, such as deciding whether or not to lease a syndicated program. Most ratings and other syndicated research reports, like Claritas Inc, Simmons Market Research and Nielsen Media Research, provide descriptions of the samples, details of the method and other information, but increasingly these descriptions are available on the companies' Web pages. For example, you can find details about how ratings are conducted at the rating services' Web sites along with a "profile of the sample" in each online report.

Table 26.1
KADLEC REPORT TABLE OF CONTENTS
(Used by permission of Kadlec Medical Center)

A Survey of the Market Served by Kadlec Medical Center

TABLE OF CONTENTS

EXAMPLES OF MAJOR REPORT ELEMENTS

The table of contents for a Kadlec Medical Center survey report (Table 26.1) illustrates the sections that should be included in a full report. Given the large number of questions in their questionnaire, it would have been possible to generate hundreds of tables, especially the "results by subgroups." However, because the project focused on specific research questions, the only results reported are those directly applicable to their RQs.

Table 26.2 is an example "executive summary" and Table 26.3 is an example "method" section, both from that same Kadlec report.

Table 26.2
KADLEC REPORT EXECUTIVE SUMMARY
(Used by permission of Kadlec Medical Center)

A Survey of the Market Served by Kadlec Medical Center

Executive Summary

Telephone interviews were conducted with 350 adult residents of the Tri-City area, 155 in Kennewick, 65 in Pasco and 130 in Richland. The interview assessed the respondent's hospital usage, health care issues, ratings of the three largest Tri-City area hospitals, hospital information sources, advertising awareness and evaluation, and Kadlec Medical Center-specific use and evaluations. Interviews were conducted during the last week of April 1992. Here are highlights of the study.

- People's primary health care concerns relate to the availability of health care in the future, cost and access to doctors.

- The primary criteria for selecting a hospital are having qualified physicians and having modern equipment. Kadlec Medical Center rates highly in those areas.

- Kadlec Medical Center offers good service because people who have had contact with the hospital, such as the emergency room, rate it higher than those who haven't.

- People get most of their information through direct contact with other people. Kadlec Medical Center needs to initiate some of this contact, reaching into the community at community meetings, workshops, church groups, etc.

- Kadlec Medical Center needs to improve in the public's perceptions of its compassion for people, planning for the future and being a good member of the community. Programs should stress this (without ignoring Kadlec Medical Center's strong staff and up-to-date equipment) and make it a part of reaching into the community.

- All three hospitals are in the same boat, facing the same people who have the same concerns for the future. Cooperation among the hospitals can help all three.

Overall, the picture of Kadlec Medical Center that is drawn by this study is a hospital that is competent with qualified staff and modern equipment, but it needs to deal more directly with people, demonstrate compassion and develop a membership in the community. Kadlec Medical Center must keep in mind that the future concern of people is whether health care will be available at a reasonable cost.

Table 26.3
KADLEC REPORT METHOD
(Used by permission of Kadlec Medical Center)

Details of the Method

Sampling. A stratified random sample of telephone numbers was selected from the most recent Tri-City area telephone book. Only numbers with addresses in Kennewick, Pasco or Richland were used. Numbers were placed on call sheets for the interviewers, and the call sheets were randomly ordered. In order to proportion the sample to parallel the populations of each city, a ratio of about 45 percent, 20 percent and 35 percent completed interviews was maintained for the three-city area, respectively, throughout the interview time period.

Questionnaire. A customized questionnaire was developed by Reagan Market Research (RMR) in consultation with the communications consultant who worked with Kadlec's staff.

The questionnaire gathered information about hospital usage, health care issues, ratings of the three Tri-City area hospitals, hospital information sources including newsletters and media, advertising awareness and evaluation, and specific questions about Kadlec use and evaluations. The demographics collected were length of residence, education, city of employment, residential zip code, income and gender. The questionnaire was pretested with a random sample of sixteen residents of the Tri-City area by telephone April 12-14. The revised questionnaire was used in this study. A copy of the questionnaire is included in the back pocket of the binder of this report.

Data collection. Interviews were conducted from phone banks at Inland Market Research located in Spokane, WA. The interviewers were trained for an hour, role-played the interview process, and were supervised. In addition, verification was done by monitoring calls on all evenings by RMR. All procedures and training were under the direction of Joey Reagan. Interviews were conducted between 6:30 and 9:30 p.m., April 24 through 31, 1992, excluding Friday and Saturday.

Response rate. Response rate is figured by taking the total number of legitimate contacts as the base (which excludes business and other nonresidential contacts) and dividing into it the total number of completions. Of the 515 residential contacts there were 350 completed interviews for a response rate of 68.0 percent. There were 155 completed interviews in Kennewick, 65 in Pasco and 130 in Richland which produces sample proportions of 44.3 percent, 18.6 percent and 37.1 percent for the three-city area, which are within sampling error of our target proportions for the three-city area.

Sampling error. Keep in mind that all numbers in this report contain "sampling error." Each number is an estimate that has an associated range of error depending upon the sample size.

For the total sample of 350 the maximum sampling error is plus or minus 5.2 percent (at a confidence level of 95 percent). The error may be lower depending on the actual results. For example, the estimate that 2.6 percent of the sample have less than a high school education has an error of plus or minus 1.7 percent, or the "true population value" that we are trying to estimate from the sample most likely falls in the range 0.9 percent to 4.3 percent.

As the sample size decreases, the sampling error increases, as in estimates for any of the subgroups. For estimates from the Kennewick subsample of 155 the maximum error is plus or minus 7.9 percent.

Sampling error also varies as the number of people answering a question changes. For example, sampling error gets larger if part of the sample does not answer a question because they do not do the activity or because they refuse or cannot answer a question. Rather than focusing on all of these sampling errors, the most important concept to keep in mind is that all of the numbers in this report are estimates and should not be treated as if they are exact.

Representativeness. Demographics for which there are population estimates from other sources including census and syndicated data (gender, income and education) are within sampling error (5.2 percent) for population demographics. This provides a basis for confidence that the sample represents the population.

JOEY REAGAN

ORAL PRESENTATION OF STUDY RESULTS

In almost all custom research, the person who is most familiar with the study and its results (usually a research director or consultant) should present a summary of the project to people who will be likely to use the results to make decisions. This usually includes the board of directors, executive committees, marketing experts, creative people or other interested groups.

The value of the oral presentation is that people who are less familiar with the study and lack research expertise can ask questions to clarify or to interpret findings and conclusions. The presentation can also raise issues that were not covered in the report and suggest additional analyses to be conducted.

CHAPTER 27

EXAMPLES OF
RESEARCH APPLICATIONS

T housands of possible applications are possible for the various techniques you
have learned about. These break down into two major areas: *syndicated research*
and *custom research*. The former is conducted on a regular schedule by companies
that store the results and sell them to many clients. This includes television ratings
that are collected in some markets on a weekly basis and sold to stations and
advertisers and agencies to help them buy and sell advertising. Custom research is
conducted by an organization or by a consultant to answer specific questions not
covered by syndicated providers, such as a survey of local buying habits.

The examples in this chapter are not designed to teach you how to apply these
studies to promotion campaigns, or sales or marketing, *per se*, but to help you
understand the variety of ways that research methods are used to help professionals.
Independent research is conducted by a company or consultant without ties to the
organization commissioning the research. It is often important to have independent
research so that others (advertising clients, agencies, etc.) trust the results.

EXAMPLES OF SYNDICATED RESEARCH

Syndicated research covers a host of applications that the media, advertisers,
program directors and others need. It documents audiences, media habits, buying
habits, product attributes, people's values, Internet click-throughs, etc. Thus,

Figure 27.1
THE NIELSEN PEOPLE METER AND DIARY

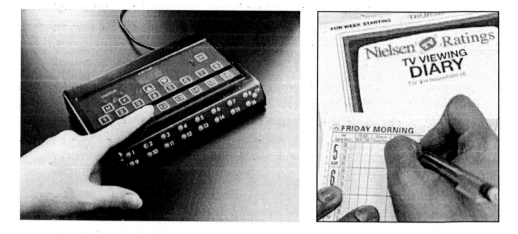

advertisers can buy programming with confidence that the viewers are in their target; those buying newspaper space can trust that the claimed subscription is correct; and TV program directors can schedule programs to match various target populations' habits.

Probably the most well-known syndicated research service is ratings, conducted by two major services in the United States, Nielsen and Arbitron. There also are a few smaller companies that serve areas that don't get good coverage by the major ratings services. Ratings are used by the media to help with programming decisions. Broadcasters, program producers, and those wanting access to the media audiences (media buyers and advertisers) also use ratings. Each is interested in audience size because that determines the rates for advertising, but the make-up of the audience is also important for targeting specific population segments; i.e., stations and networks can decide which programs to create, retain or drop.

Nielsen Media Research (Nielsen) conducts television audience research. Nielsen uses both electronic "people meters" and mail diaries (see Figure 27.1). The "National People Meter" provides audience estimates for broadcast network programs, cable networks, Spanish language networks and nationally syndicated programs.

The National Nielsen, used for national ratings, uses a sample of about 5,000 households. A meter is connected to each TV set and measures two things: the program or channel tuned to and who is watching. Using remote controls, each family member logs in. Data are stored in the metering system and are retrieved by

Nielsen computers each night. Thus, daily reports are available to subscribers.

Sampling is done by first using the Census Bureau's counts of all housing units in the nation and then randomly selecting about 6,000 small geographic areas (blocks in urban areas and their equivalent in rural areas). Then "surveyors" go to each area to list housing units. Housing units are randomly selected within each sample area. Each occupied housing unit is a household. These are stratified to represent geographic areas.

Local ratings use a mix of meters and diaries. Of the 210 local U.S. markets, the largest 56 use meters and the rest use paper diaries. For electronic local markets, about 400 to 500 households are used (not the same homes as the national sample). In the other 154 local markets, a diary is used in November, February, May and July of each year. Hence, Nielsen uses multiple methods for gathering TV viewing information:

- Two research designs, panel and trend. Panels are the electronic households that are monitored continuously. Trends use the paper diaries that are sent to different households for each survey period.
- Multi-stage sampling methods. First using a frame of geographic areas and selecting a subset of those areas, then creating their own frame by enumerating the living units and then randomly selecting from that frame.
- Different sample sizes. 5,000 households for national people meters and 400 to 500 for local ratings.

Coincidental studies are a form of ratings research, but they are usually done as custom research, sometimes by ratings companies and sometimes by a station or programmer. These studies take place at the same time as people are watching or listening ("coincidental" with people's media use). The design is a cross-sectional survey with a very short questionnaire.

However, large samples may be used to make sure people watching low-rated programs (those with less than 1 percent audience) have a chance to be contacted. Respondents are telephoned and simply asked, "Are you watching TV right now?" and, if so, "What channel are you watching?" This can also be used for radio listening.

This type of research is especially useful for specialized programming that does not appear in traditional ratings, where, overall, the number of people watching TV is low, where there is fragmentation of the audience as with cable and satellite TV, or where programming appears outside the weeks when ratings are conducted, such as local high school football telecasts.

Claritas Inc. is a target-marketing information company. The information helps with business-to-business marketing and business-to-consumer marketing.

One of the company's products is "Claritas Cable," which gathers information about all cable systems, including number of subscribers, channels in use, and number of local ad channels available. This allows you to verify that your ad placement reaches the published number of subscribers.

It provides consumer information with PRIZM NE, a segmentation system that allows you to target narrow population segments. Claritas combines information from various databases, including the census, county data, their own financial surveys, Polk car buyer surveys, and Media Mark surveys. These data cover almost 90 percent of U.S. households and are classified into social and lifestyle groups.

Suppose you wanted to know about people in the Atlanta, Georgia, ZIP code 30305. PRIZM NE describes that segment of people as "Executive Suites, Movers & Shakers, Old Glories, Upper Crust and Young Influentials." Extensive descriptions of each segment are also provided, such as:

> Executive Suites consists of upper-middle-class singles and couples typically living just beyond the nation's beltways. Filled with significant numbers of Asian Americans and college graduates — both groups are represented at more than twice the national average — this segment is a haven for white-collar professionals drawn to comfortable homes and apartments within a manageable commute to downtown jobs, restaurants and entertainment. (Used by permission of Claritas Inc.)

The service also provides demographics and lifestyle traits, allowing you to target not only who is in the segments but also how and where they shop, what media they use and their attitudes. Like Nielsen, Claritas also uses multiple techniques:

- Census for business information (e.g., a census of all cable systems).
- Survey (e.g., consumer surveys to assess demographics, lifestyle, etc.).

There are many other syndicated providers. Audit Bureau of Circulations, which verifies circulation for print publications (including inserts and locations), paid and nonpaid circulation, and reader profiles. Simmons Market Research profiles consumer product and media usage, reporting on 8,000 brands in 450 product categories. The survey covers everything from "frozen hot snacks" to "packaged dry dog food."

EXAMPLES OF CUSTOM RESEARCH

Obviously, syndicated research cannot provide information for needs that are peculiar to a specific market or problem, or to issues that arise unexpectedly. So you may find yourself needing *custom research*, research that is tailor-made for your specific needs and goals.

Custom research can be conducted by various entities: syndicated research providers, small research companies and consultants. If it's not very complicated, you can do it yourself, called *in-house research*. Large companies, such as Microsoft and Coca Cola, have their own research departments or research directors, although they may also hire independent research companies or *vendors* to do parts of studies like data collection. Finally, there is the option to hire research companies or consultants to conduct all of the research. The following are two examples of custom research.

ANNE ELLEN'S COOKIES

This example involves in-house research that does a taste test using a convenience sample. Anne Ellen's Cookies was a small local company and had developed several kinds of low-fat and nonfat cookies: chocolate chip, snickerdoodle, and other varieties. Anne needed to find out if the taste of her cookies was substitutable for the typical high-fat ones. The RQ was, "Is there a difference in the taste of Anne Ellen's cookies and the same type of regular cookie?" Anne, of course, was hoping there wasn't. Clearly, the only way to find out was to have people taste an Anne Ellen's cookie and compare it to one of their own brand.

The preferred method would be a cross-sectional survey with a random sample of people in her market, in-person. You could deliver cookies to a random sample by mail or another delivery system and follow-up with a mail or phone questionnaire, but there would be problems with cookies getting stale or crushed unless expensive packaging was used.

However, Anne could not afford the preferred method, so she used a convenience sample at locations where people find specialty cookies: a university cafeteria, a retirement home dining room and a coffee shop. Anne hired a consultant to design the study, train the interviewers, conduct the analysis and write the report. Her employees gathered the data.

The results showed that people found the Anne Ellen's cookie tasted equal to or better than existing brands. This study also agreed with national research which showed that although people may want lower fat or natural ingredients, the most important consideration is the taste of the cookie. Confident about the cookie taste, Anne could turn to using taste as the primary advertising strategy to promote her cookies.

KADLEC MEDICAL CENTER

This is an example of a trend study to track hospital issues. It was a trend because the same questions were asked with two different samples in two years, 1993 and 1994. Kadlec Medical Center, located in central Washington State, found itself in competition with the two other local hospitals and hospitals in Seattle. While national research suggested that bedside manner and other factors were important in people's selection of a hospital, Kadlec had no definitive research to identify these or other factors as important to the local population. So they formulated several research questions, among which were: "What are the most important factors people use in deciding which hospital to go to?", "What are the important local healthcare issues?" and "What sources do people use for information about the local hospitals?"

In 1993, Kadlec hired a consultant who conducted a telephone survey based on a systematic random sample of local phone numbers. The questionnaire included both closed- and open-ended questions. Results showed that:

- The most important local healthcare issues were cost and doctor availability.
- The most important factors for selecting a hospital were "having qualified physicians" and "having modern equipment."
- Friends, neighbors and other people were the major sources of information about hospitals (cited by 46 percent of the sample), much higher than doctors (29 percent). (Used by permission of Kadlec Medical Center)

Of course, the results could be idiosyncratic to the issues of that time period (e.g., the local economy), so to confirm the results a replication was conducted in 1994. It corroborated the importance of hospital selection factors and "friends and neighbors, and other people" as the main information source. It also found even more people concerned with "an adequate supply of doctors" as a local healthcare issue.

Based on the results several strategies were pursued to more effectively

Figure 27.2

PART OF THE FRONT PAGE OF KADLEC MEDICAL CENTER'S *PACESETTER*

(Used by permission of Kadlec Medical Center)

PACESETTER

Sharing ideas for healthy lifestyles

November 2005   Volume 17, Issue 3

Expanding the Region's Neurological Care

When Matthew Fewel, MD, was looking at locations to establish his neurosurgery practice, a key factor was Kadlec Medical Center's commitment to strengthen the neurological care services available in the region.

"Kadlec was clear in its desire to develop and expand neurosciences in the area," said Dr. Fewel. "I could see that the population could support additional neurosurgeons and I wanted to work at a hospital that supported that growth potential. I knew that Kadlec had been aggressive in developing key services for the community in the past with the heart program a prime example. The commit-

ment to expanding neuroservices is just as strong."

Kadlec's president and chief executive officer concurs. "We intend to recruit neurosurgeons until we are able to provide the region with full-time neurosurgery coverage," said Rand Wortman. "We think this is an important service the Tri-Cities area does not currently have."

In order to achieve that goal, a neurosciences program at Kadlec needs to draw from the communities that make up the Tri-Cities, but also "from a large geographical area," said Wortman. "The more regional Kadlec is able to become, the more we can then attract additional

neurosurgeons to provide that full-time coverage that this region needs."

The commitment to neurosurgery at Kadlec also extends to securing equipment needed by the neurosurgeons in order to support and expand their practices. "Kadlec has been more than helpful in providing the technology and equipment we need. One example is the addition of the latest image-guided surgery system. It is cutting-edge technology," said Dr. Fewel.

Dr. Fewel joins Drs. Anjan Sen and Thomas Wilkinson as the area's neurosurgeons. Neurologists on the active Kadlec medical staff are Drs. Daniel Washington and Hui-Juan Zhang.

place promotion and to tailor the content of that promotion to match local healthcare issues and factors affecting hospital selection. Specifically, the strategies were:

- To promote to people as directly as possible through newsletters, community centers, seminars, etc. to capitalize on friends and neighbors as the major source of information.
- To focus the content of the promotion on the cutting edge technology and competency of staff.
- To recruit doctors to the area, and to publicize that effort.

Figure 27.2 shows the *Pacesetter* newsletter which promotes to people directly by being sent to residents and handed out or left behind when meeting groups in the community. It emphasizes the competent staff and having the latest technologies.

Many other useful findings helped Kadlec effectively prepare promotion and community interaction. To this day Kadlec continues to monitor the market with surveys and on-site interviews with hospital visitors and patients in order to monitor trends in the local healthcare market.

OTHER RESEARCH APPLICATIONS

Obviously, whole books can be written about research applications. The following is a short summary of some of the more important types.

Evaluation research is anything that helps you determine whether your campaign, promotions, interventions or other communications are successful, along with what factors were important in its success or failure (or partial success).

A *benchmark study* is a first project against which future studies are compared. Important variables are selected, based on your needs, that are replicated in the future studies. Changes in those variables help you infer whether your strategies were correct. Sales change is an obvious example, but you may want to evaluate whether the placement of your ad was correct, requiring variables to assess media use and attention to ads. Many areas can be evaluated:

- Was the placement correct, both media and time period?
- What contexts helped or hindered — weather, news, etc.?
- Are specific outcomes achieved? Sales goals, revenue, image changes, etc.?

Return on investment (ROI) techniques seek to quantify the dollar impact of campaigns. This may easily be done if store traffic or sales are used and compared to the cost of creating and running a campaign. Research, of course, is one component of the cost of developing a campaign. Added to research is campaign development, media costs and overhead. Simply subtract the costs from the increased revenues.

However, public relations and other campaigns can be much more difficult to justify using ROI techniques. Projecting how improved image and other factors affect sales can be done but it is difficult.

Outcome research is used to measure effects or changes based on predefined criteria. (Some managers call this "evidence-based," "output-based" or "outcome-based PR"). For example, you might ask, "Has there been a change in attitudes?" or "Has there been a change in behavior?" Some people just view PR as a necessary cost and do not try to account for the costs of its implementation.

Formative research evaluates the strength of campaign materials before or during the campaign's implementation. It usually involves qualitative or a combination of qualitative and quantitative designs to discover the interests and needs of the target, what gets their attention and what messages resonate with them.

Internal communication studies try to evaluate the quality or effectiveness of communication within organizations. The usual design is a survey, although other designs like in-depth interviews can be used.

Media monitoring tracks the coverage of your company or personnel by radio, TV, newspapers, the Internet, and other media. Various techniques are used for tracking, most of them focusing on searches for specific terms like "XYZ Company." Companies who do tracking then provide transcripts, tapes, DVDs and other reports of the coverage.

There are many other types of research, such as *process research* which measures how much was accomplished like the number people reached and *impact research* which measures longer-term results such as changes in sales over months and years.

CHAPTER 28

RESEARCH ETHICS

T here is no law requiring market researchers to tell the truth (except when there is fraud). Nobody licenses research consultants. There is no "Federal Research Administration" that reviews research and research practices.

There are many examples of abuse in the name of science. Most well-known, perhaps, are the medical experiments conducted on unconsenting people during World War II. In the 1960s, medical research into hepatitis was conducted on mentally retarded children.

Less well known are experiments in the social sciences, such as the "Stanford Prison Experiment" in 1971, which many researchers believe were unethical. People were randomly assigned to be "prisoners" or "guards." The experiment did not anticipate how sadistic the guards would be. The prisoners were humiliated and many showed emotional distress but were pressured to remain in the experiment.

Even without the obvious abuses described above, researchers can offend people, embarrass them or invade their privacy.

Imagine, for example, if you participated in a survey about your sexual habits. Would you be uncomfortable if you were asked about infantilism? What if someone asked about sexual activity while interviewing your 12-year-old son or daughter? Would you want a researcher asking you about your income and political attitudes, and then put your name and your answers into a database or a report that was available to other people?

ETHICS IN ACADEMIA

Practices like those described above have led to tighter scrutiny of academic research. Arising out of this were federal laws and guidelines that govern research in academia and in organizations where federal funds are used. Institutional guidelines and the publication process itself help ensure that most academic research is ethical.

Ethics are the guidelines in which researchers work. The purpose of these guidelines is to pose the least risk to society. While there are some legal aspects to ethics, most guidelines are developed by professional associations and institutions where scientists work.

For example, The American Psychological Association's (APA) Web site provides a thorough review of social science research ethics. This review provides both guidelines for ethics and the legal requirements imposed by the federal government for funded research. However, their sanctions are limited to informal resolution or expulsion from the association. The APA's basic tenets for researchers include:

- Benefit those with whom they work and do no harm.
- Accuracy, honesty, and truthfulness in science.
- Respect the dignity and worth of all people.

This theme runs through most academic ethics guides. That is, (1) the research should be good scientific research designed to benefit society, (2) it should do no harm to people, obviously no physical harm, but it should also do no psychological harm, (3) the research should be honest, and (4) it should respect all people.

Legal requirements have been adopted by the federal government to impose ethics upon researchers. These requirements are intended to protect people who participate in research. The Public Health Services Act (Title 42 of the U.S. Code), under which the Department of Health and Human Services regulates research, and the 1979 Belmont Report, "Ethical Principles and Guidelines for the Protection of Human Subjects of Research," provide the basis of that protection. This is usually referred to as "Protection of Human Subjects." All entities (e.g., universities) that receive federal research money, inside or outside of academia, must submit research proposals to a "human subjects review" to make certain that the research meets scientific standards, benefits society and does not expose people to unnecessary risk.

Institutional policies also regulate what employees and others working with the institution can do. Washington State University, for example, has its own policies that implement and extend the legal requirements. These include:

- Subject safety and rights are maintained.
- Risks to subjects are minimized.
- Risks to subjects are justified in relation to anticipated benefits.
- The selection of subjects is equitable.
- Subjects will be informed of all procedures, costs, risks, and benefits of participating in a research study.

Informed consent is an essential element of "human subjects review." That is, subjects in an experiment or interviewees for a survey have a right to know what the study is about, what the risks are, how their privacy will be protected and that their participation is voluntary.

If institutions discover their procedures have not been followed, they can require scientists to stop their research, confiscate data and impose other sanctions.

Peer review helps ensure trustworthy research by using eminent scientists in a field to critically appraise the research of their colleagues before that research is published or "absorbed" into the field. Usually, this takes the form of an editorial board for a journal that critiques submitted research reports. The purpose is twofold. First, the peer review makes sure that the researcher is using appropriate scientific methods; if the science is not good then no risk is acceptable. Second, it determines if the research has moved the field forward; that is, has it benefitted science and simultaneously benefitted society?

ETHICS OUTSIDE ACADEMIA

While procedures and requirements within academia help ensure ethical research, the professional world does not have the same standards. Researchers who receive federal funding, including independent consultants, corporations and nonprofits, must comply with federal law about protecting human subjects, but most professional research is privately funded and not subject to those reviews. Thus, they are free to conduct research in almost any manner they wish. Still, there are methods for enforcing standards.

Contracts provide a legal basis for ensuring good research practices. For example, you can include in your contract with a consultant how large a sample to use. Even so, you cannot include every detail of a research project in a contract; so you must trust your consultant or research department. That trust usually comes from their professionalism and track record.

Professionalism is the reputation earned by the researcher because they have a good track record and professional credentials. You should check on the track record by always checking references. Professional credentials accrue from training. You can find out if their degree comes from an institution that teaches ethics, their memberships, and the ethics policies and enforcement procedures for the associations they belong to.

The American Association for Public Opinion Research (AAPOR) is a large organization for academic and professional public opinion researchers, many research companies belong to it. AAPOR has a set of principles that its members agree to before joining. AAPOR will "dismember" violators. Table 28.1 lists those principles.

Good research is good business. Being an ethical researcher is good promotion for the company. Conducting good research provides the client with good data. The client then makes good decisions and is happy. A happy client is more likely to be a repeat client and to recommend a researcher to a colleague.

Making the researcher aware you are concerned with ethics and how research is conducted avoids problems, and, of course, acting ethically yourself and expecting ethical professional work will set the tone. *Caveat emptor;* it's up to you to ensure that your research is ethically done and of high quality.

SPECIAL ISSUES FOR ONLINE RESEARCH

The increasing use of electronic data-gathering opens new areas of concern, most of which relate to privacy. For example, in a telephone survey it is easy to just use an RDD sample and simply not include the phone number in the database or spreadsheet when the study is over, and in a mail survey you just use a return envelope without the subject's return address on it; but when you use e-mail to send and receive a questionnaire, the e-mail address is attached to the return. You have to deliberately remove the e-mail address to ensure that no identifying information is included. Other problems with online research include:

- People's behavior can easily be tracked using cookies.
- Some people are unaware that their electronic behavior is not private.
- Information protected in one part of the world may not be protected in another.
- Recording illegal activity is possible.
- Sexual and other sensitive activity may be disclosed.
- Tracking back to individuals, even when using pseudonyms, is easy.
- Access to minors is easy.

JOEY REAGAN

Table 28.1
AAPOR RESEARCH PRINCIPLES
(Used by permission of American Association for Public Opinion Research)

I. Principles of Professional Practice in the Conduct of Our Work

A. We shall exercise due care in developing research designs and survey instruments, and in collecting, processing, and analyzing data, taking all reasonable steps to assure the reliability and validity of results.
1. We shall recommend and employ only those tools and methods of analysis which, in our professional judgment, are well suited to the research problem at hand.
2. We shall not select research tools and methods of analysis because of their capacity to yield misleading conclusions.
3. We shall not knowingly make interpretations of research results, nor shall we be tacitly permit interpretations, that are inconsistent with the data available.
4. We shall not knowingly imply that interpretations should be accorded greater confidence than the data actually warrant.
B. We shall describe our methods and findings accurately and in appropriate detail in all research reports, adhering to the standards for minimal disclosure specified in Section III.
C. If any of our work becomes the subject of a formal investigation of an alleged violation of this Code, undertaken with the approval of the AAPOR Executive Council, we shall provide additional information on the survey in such detail that a fellow survey practitioner would be able to conduct a professional evaluation of the survey.

II. Principles of Professional Responsibility in Our Dealings With People

A. The Public:
1. If we become aware of the appearance in public of serious distortions of our research, we shall publicly disclose what is required to correct these distortions, including, as appropriate, a statement to the public media, legislative body, regulatory agency, or other appropriate group, in or before which the distorted findings were presented.
B. Clients or Sponsors:
1. When undertaking work for a private client, we shall hold confidential all proprietary information obtained about the client and about the conduct and findings of the research undertaken for the client, except when the dissemination of the information is expressly authorized by the client, or when disclosure becomes necessary under terms of Section I-C or II-A of this Code.
2. We shall be mindful of the limitations of our techniques and capabilities and shall accept only those research assignments which we can reasonably expect to accomplish within these limitations.
C. The Profession:
1. We recognize our responsibility to contribute to the science of public opinion research and to disseminate as freely as possible the ideas and findings which emerge from our research.
2. We shall not cite our membership in the Association as evidence of professional competence, since the Association does not so certify any persons or organizations.
D. The Respondent:
1. We shall strive to avoid the use of practices or methods that may harm, humiliate, or seriously mislead survey respondents.
2. Unless the respondent waives confidentiality for specified uses, we shall hold as privileged and confidential all information that might identify a respondent with his or her responses. We shall also not disclose or use the names of respondents for non-research purposes unless the respondents grant us permission to do so.

Table 28.1 (continued)
AAPOR RESEARCH PRINCIPLES

III. Standard for Minimal Disclosure

Good professional practice imposes the obligation upon all public opinion researchers to include, in any report of research results, or to make available when that report is released, certain essential information about how the research was conducted. At a minimum, the following items should be disclosed:

1. Who sponsored the survey, and who conducted it.
2. The exact wording of questions asked, including the text of any preceding instruction or explanation to the interviewer or respondents that might reasonably be expected to affect the response.
3. A definition of the population under study, and a description of the sampling frame used to identify this population.
4. A description of the sample selection procedure, giving a clear indication of the method by which the respondents were selected by the researcher, or whether the respondents were entirely self-selected.
5. Size of samples and, if applicable, completion rates and information on eligibility criteria and screening procedures.
6. A discussion of the precision of the findings, including, if appropriate, estimates of sampling error, and a description of any weighting or estimating procedures used.
7. Which results are based on parts of the sample, rather than on the total sample.
8. Method, location, and dates of data collection.

- There are problems with accuracy, especially tracking the attribution of statements and facts.
- Researchers can disrupt the environment in new ways. Participation in chats and other electronic environments can affect how people act in ethnographic research.

CHAPTER 29

GETTING HELP FROM
CONSULTANTS & OTHER SOURCES

U nless you get advanced training in statistics and research, you normally will need to get help to do your research project. Whether you hire an outside consultant, work with your company's research department or work on your own, you may need help with complicated designs or analyses. Thus, you will need to access information in books or online to get ideas for studies, look up cases, refresh your knowledge of statistical tests or find other information.

CONSULTANTS

Like any business, there are great, mediocre and lousy researchers. Since there is no licensing of research providers, having some knowledge of research will help you find a good one.

Of course, there is the basic information: How long have they been in business? Do they have references? But there are special questions you need to ask to verify that a consultant is qualified. Even if the consultant is very competent, knowing that you are on top of things will make them pay more attention to details of the project, including ethical concerns, so ask questions during your initial consultations; ask consultants the same questions you would ask yourself as you plan various parts of the study, such as:

- How do they plan to measure variables? Why?
- How will they develop the questionnaire? Why?
- What design and data-gathering technique will they use? Why?
- What sample size do they recommend? Why?
- What is the expected sampling error?
- What analysis will they provide?

In addition, your consultant or research director should provide you with the following services which should be included in your contract:

- Within reason, additional analyses based on questions that come up after the final report and presentation
- Copies of all creations for the project: questionnaire, DVDs and transcripts, mock ups, etc.
- Copies of the codebook and data file

The burden is on you to ascertain whether the consultant you hire is reputable. You should be wary of consultants if they:

- Only know a narrow range of methodologies
- Recommend research but do not follow the process in Chapter 3
- Use a lot of jargon, especially inappropriately
- Suggest questionnaire items without pretesting
- Develop questions or scales with language not generated by your target population
- Use very large samples
- Use nonrandom samples and tell you they're the same as random samples
- Don't do things your way
- Have no processes for verification
- Conduct a study their way because "that's the way we always do it"
- Tell you research is the answer (not a tool)

If the consultant doesn't follow the procedures you have learned in this book, find out why. In the end, it is your responsibility to ensure that the study is done correctly.

WHERE DO YOU FIND CONSULTANTS?

They can be found in many places: the phone book, on the Internet, through colleague recommendations and from professional associations. Professional associations offer seminars on research. Their conventions often include panels reporting research and workshops on research and analysis. The people making those presentations may be valuable contacts as possible consultants.

Universities can offer you inexpensive and competent help. Universities are full of people who do research and who teach research methods and statistics classes. The trick is to find someone familiar with applied research who can guarantee the data collection will be high quality even though done by students. The university and the professor benefit by getting credit for a grant and you benefit by saving money while getting trustworthy research. The only drawback is that public university research is public information. That is, anyone can request access to a study. Thus, your competitors may have access to your research if they find out you're doing it. However, the data will be proprietary if the professor hires a private company to field the survey.

INFORMATION SOURCES

A variety of helpful sources exist, including Web pages from professional organizations, books on research design, books on statistics and consultants' Web pages.

While I have found the following resources to be helpful, I do not necessarily recommend them over other sources not listed. There are many good suppliers, and you are encouraged to search for them yourself. For example, a search of Amazon.com with keywords like "communication research" and "advertising research" will result in numerous books and reviews. Sage Publications has several series of books devoted to research, with individual books devoted specifically to focus groups, sampling and advanced statistics.

Keep in mind that the basics of research are the same whether you are a public relations professional, advertiser or broadcaster, so you can pick up valuable tips from many different sources. Much of the online information is free, but books and other proprietary resources require purchase, fee or membership.

Professional organizations are excellent sources offering research tips, books, video tapes, CDs, DVDs and online help. Each organization has scores more resources than listed here.

- Public Relations Society of America (www.prsa.org) has:

  ‣ RFP (Request For Proposals) Exchange where you can post a request for a research project
  ‣ E-Learning Center with seminars like "Measuring Public Relations Effectiveness: Research and Evaluation"

- Professional Resource Center with winning campaign case studies and other information

- International Association of Business Communicators (www.iabc.com) offers:

  - Printed and "pdf" publications like the *Communication Research Primer* by Joey Reagan
  - Seminars on various communication topics, on the Web and at conferences
  - Gold Quill Winning Workplans that demonstrate applications to numerous communication problems

- American Association for Public Opinion Research (www.aapor.org) offers research method tips and several papers on the characteristics of good surveys and pitfalls of research, including:

  - "Code of Professional Ethics" used in this book
  - "Best Practices for Research," a guide to determining if a study is scientific
  - What constitutes a "scientific" survey
  - Precautions for Web-based surveys
  - Calculations and explanations of outcome rates
  - International list of research companies and consultants

- National Association of Broadcasters (www.nab.org) offers publications about conducting research and the place of research in management. It has a Research and Information Division. The NAB provides:

  - Tracking of ratings response rates
  - Updates on new research technologies like the Personal People Meter
  - *Troubleshooting Audience Research* by Walter McDowell
  - *Audience Research Sourcebook by* Gerald Hartshorn

- American Association of Advertising Agencies (www.aaaa.org) publishes:

  - *A Guide to AAAA Research Services*
  - *Guide to Media Research*
  - Links to advertising industry associations

- The World Advertising Research Center (www.warc.com) has:

  - A database of case studies
  - Statistics articles
  - Published papers on international research such as "Life cycle, objective and subjective living standards and life satisfaction. New indexes building and applications, Poland"

- Nielsen Media Research (www.nielsenmedia.com) has:

  - Description of methods such as "Sampling & Recruiting"
  - Articles on measurement issues like "Metering Televisions in the Digital Age"

- The American Marketing Association (www.marketingpower.com) has many offerings on research strategies in electronic and print form:

  - Marketing trade publications including *Marketing News* and *Marketing Research*
  - Books like *Marketing Scales Handbook, Volume I, A Compilation of Multi-Item Measures* by Gordon C. Bruner and Paul J. Hensel
  - A search engine allowing advanced searches for consultants
  - A section called Best Practices in Research, which includes "Selecting a Market Research Supplier"

On-line media sources number in the hundreds. They range from the traditional companies like Nielsen NetRatings that track usage and consumer behavior to Jupiter Communications, which, in addition to tracking Web use, also tries to assess the effect of online scams and attacks to see why users do not make online purchases. Each provides background on their research techniques on their Web pages.

An especially good resource for general population political and social attitudes is The Pew Research Center for the People and the Press (http://people-press.org). They have hundreds of studies available online, and they provide the exact questionnaires, descriptions of methods and results (frequencies, percentages and verbatim categories).

Traditional research books are always good resources, especially if you need specialized and in-depth information. There are hundreds of research textbooks and manuals. The bibliography on the next page provides a good reference library for basic and advanced statistics, research methods and applying research to business communication.

Selected Bibliography

Erica Weintraub Austin and Bruce E. Pinkleton, *Strategic Public Relations Management: Planning and Managing Effective Communication Programs*, 2nd ed. (Mahwah, NJ: Lawrence Erlbaum Associates, 2006).

Earl Babbie. *The Practice of Social Research*, 11th ed. (Belmont, CA: Thomson Wadsworth, 2007).

Hubert M. Blalock, Jr. , *Social Statistics*, 2nd ed. (New York: McGraw-Hill, 1979).

Glen M. Broom and David M. Dozier, *Using Research in Public Relations* (Englewood Cliffs, NJ: Prentice-Hall, 1990).

Jacob Cohen and Patricia Cohen, *Applied Multiple Regression/Correlation Analysis for the Behavioral Sciences*, 3rd ed. (Mahwah, NJ: Lawrence Erlbaum Associates, 2003).

David Demers and Susan Nichols, *Precision Journalism: A Practical Guide* (Newbury Park, CA: Sage, 1987).

Don A. Dillman, *Mail and Internet Surveys: The Tailored Design Method*, 2nd ed. (New York: Wiley, 2000).

William L. Hays, *Statistics*, 5th ed. (Fort Worth, TX: Harcourt College Publishers, 1994)

Kimberly A. Neuendorf, *The Content Analysis Guidebook* (Thousand Oaks, CA: Sage, 2002).

James Stevens, *Applied Multivariate Statistics for the Social Sciences*, 4th ed. (Mahwah, NJ: Lawrence Erlbaum Associates, 2002).

Roger D. Wimmer and Joseph R. Dominick, *Mass Media Research: An Introduction*, 8th ed. (Belmont, CA: Thomson Wadsworth, 2006).

GLOSSARY

accuracy How close a measure can get to a true observation. The amount of error in a measure. *See*: precision.

authority The basis for explaining how the world works because of trust in the source of the explanation.

bias Anything that interferes with making a rational decision.

bivariate analysis Relational analysis using exactly two variables.

case study Examining a single case or example to learn from someone who has already encountered a similar problem.

CATI Computer Assisted Telephone Interviewing. Using a computer to assist the interviewer by showing questions and responses on the screen, allowing electronic entry of responses and controlling routing.

cause-and-effect (causation) A relation such that one variable precedes the other in time and other relations can be eliminated. *See*: independent variable and dependent variable.

census A comprehensive examination of a population, using all members of the population, assessing variables for the purpose of describing or finding relations in that population.

chi-square (χ^2) Significance test for nominal or ordinal data, often used for crosstabulations.

cleaning data Performing visual checks or data analysis to find errors in data entry.

closed-ended *See*: fixed-response.

codebook A list of variables along with how those variables were operationalized and the coding of the responses.

coding Assigning numbers or categories to responses.

cohort study A longitudinal survey using a subgroup with similar characteristics (e.g., X-generationers) of a population over the time periods. *See*: longitudinal, cross-sectional, trend, and panel.

coincidental study A form of ratings research, usually custom research, conducted "coincidentally" or at the same time as people are using the medium under study.

confidence interval The number of standard deviations associated with a specific confidence level. For example, if the confidence level is .95, then the confidence interval is ±1.96sd. *See*: confidence level and sampling error.

confidence level The probability that an estimate based on a random sample is accurate. A probability associated with the normal curve. It is the probability that an event is within a certain number of standard deviations. *See*: confidence interval.

constant Something that does not vary, such as: women, 18-25 year olds, a target market, ZIP-Code 48203. *See*: variable.

construct validity The measures have been constructed well. The variable's definition has been used successfully in previous research or is based on good theory. *See*: reliability, validity, face validity, predictive validity, content validity, internal validity and external validity.

content analysis A survey (sometimes a census) of content rather than people.

content validity How much a variable matches the concept a researcher is trying to measure. *See*: reliability, validity, face validity, predictive validity, construct validity, internal validity and external validity.

control The part of an experiment that does not receive the treatment or stimulus.

convenience study Interviewing people simply because they appear at a convenient location.

correlation coefficient (correlation) A statistic ranging between "−1" and "+1" that estimates the strength and direction of a relation among interval or ratio level variables. *See*: relation.

cross-sectional survey A survey at one time period. A snapshot or "cross section" of a population. *See*: longitudinal, trend, panel and cohort.

cross-test reliability (parallel forms) A large number of items is split randomly into two halves. Each half is administered separately with the expectation that the two separate tests are highly correlated *See*: reliability, validity, predictive validity, content validity, construct validity, internal validity and external validity.

custom research Research conducted by an organization or by a consultant to answer specific questions not covered by syndicated research, such as a survey of local buying habits.

database generators Entering data into computers via electronic scanners, the Internet and other techniques in order to develop computer files that are searchable.

dependent variable (DV) In a hypothesis, or causal statement or question, it is the presumed effect.

depth interviews *See*: in-depth.

descriptive research (descriptive analysis) Using single variables to describe a population. Not trying to relate one variable to another. Common descriptors include mean, median, mode, frequencies and percentages.

electronic techniques Data collection via the Internet such as Web-based questionnaires or questionnaires sent by e-mail.

evaluation research Any research that helps determine whether campaigns, promotions, interventions or other communications are successful, along with what factors were important in success or failure (or partial success). It is longitudinal research comparing later time periods with an initial benchmark study.

exhaustive For nominal and ordinal level variables, all possible observations or responses have a category.

experiment A test of cause-and-effect with the independent variable being treatments or stimuli with a control and the dependent variable being some observation of changes in behavior, attitude, opinion or other effect variable. It also controls time order and excludes or accounts for other possible causes or independent variables.

experimental group (treatment group) In an experiment, one category of the independent variable. The receivers of a stimulus or treatment.

explained variance In relations between two or more variables, how much variability in one variable is explained or accounted for by a second variable. It estimates the strength of a relation. Some estimates of explained variance are C, η^2, and r^2.

external validity The ability to generalize to the population from which a sample was selected. *See*: reliability, validity, predictive validity, content validity, construct validity, internal validity and external validity.

face validity An argument that "on its face" the question or response categories of an operationalization appears to measure what it is supposed to measure. *See*: reliability, validity, predictive validity, content validity, construct validity, internal validity and external validity.

***F*-test for multiple means** A significance test where one variable is nominal with three or more categories and the other variable is interval or ratio.

field experiment An experiment conducted under physical conditions where the behavior being studied naturally occurs.

fixed-response (fixed-choice) A question or item whose responses are known ahead of time, are limited by logic or are specified by the researcher.

focus group Leading a group of about seven to 20 people through a dialogue or discussion, from a general discussion of a topic to a focused discussion of that topic.

formal research An attempt to gather information that is guided by a research plan.

formative research Research that assesses the strength of campaign materials before or during the campaign's implementation. It tries to discover the interests and needs of the target, what gets their attention and what messages affect them.

frame The list from which a sample is selected.

generalizability The ability to infer results from a sample to its population; the applicability of the sample to the population.

hypothesis (H) A causal statement about a relation between two variables, one of which is an *independent* variable and one of which is a *dependent* variable. Hypotheses should be deduced from a theory or body of consistent research.

hypothesis testing *See*: statistical test.

in-depth interview (depth interview) One-on-one, interviewer and interviewee, eliciting insightful responses to questions, follow-up questions and probes.

in–person interview *See:* personal interview.

index A series of items or statements with varying response categories that are totaled to get a scale score. Indexes usually assess how many or how often as opposed to scales that usually assess attitudes, opinions and other variables. *See*: scale.

informal research Gathering information without a research plan.

independent variable (IV) In a hypothesis, or causal statement or question, it is the presumed cause.

inferential statistics *See*: statistical test.

internal communication study Research that evaluates the quality or effectiveness of communication within an organization.

internal consistency A reliability measure for indexes or scales that assess how well items relate to each other.

internal validity The extent to which the results of research can be related to the variables that were used. It assesses whether there is a link between the variables and the results or to some other cause. *See*: reliability, validity, face validity, predictive validity, content validity, construct validity, internal validity and external validity.

inter-observer reliability (inter-rater reliability) The consistency between observers, raters or people who assign categories to open-ended questions or transcripts from qualitative studies.

interval level of measurement Three or more responses that have equal intervals between the responses. Scale scores are assumed to be at least interval level of measurement.

intuition The basis for explaining how the world works from a gut feeling or personal insight.

lab experiment An experiment conducted in a room or auditorium.

levels of measurement A system for determining if a measure is at the "level" that is required by an operationalization. The system moves from "categories" to "ordered categories" to "arithmetic intervals" to "real numbers." The level determines what analysis can be done along with what statistical tests and other estimates can be computed. *See*: nominal, ordinal, interval and ratio.

Likert scale A scale using statements and an odd number of responses such as "strongly agree, agree, neutral, disagree, strongly disagree."

longitudinal survey (longitudinal research). A survey conducted over two or more points in time.

mail technique Using mail, by post office or internal mail, or other method that allows physically sending a questionnaire to a respondent.

measurement How observations or responses are to be recorded, in numbers, categories or words.

media monitoring Tracking the coverage of a company or personnel by radio, TV, newspapers, the Internet, and other media.

multiple response item A question or item that allows a respondent to select more than one response.

multivariate analysis Analysis of three or more variables simultaneously. Some multivariate analyses are "linear regression," "cluster analysis," "time series analysis," "mapping," "factor analysis," "reliability" and "conjoint analysis."

mutually exclusive For nominal and ordinal level variables, observations or responses fit into only one category. Categories don't overlap.

N Sample size.

n Sub-sample size.

negative relation Two variables change together such that as one variable's values increase the other's decrease. *See*: positive relation and no relation.

no relation Among two variables, as one variable's values change the other's stay the same or change randomly. *See*: negative relation and positive relation.

nominal level of measurement Two or more response categories with separate names, not in order. A list of race categories is nominal.

nonprobability sample *See*: nonrandom sample.

nonrandom sample A sample from a population in which each member does *not* have an equal chance of being selected. Some techniques for selecting nonrandom samples are "convenience," "judgment," "quota," "snowball" and "volunteer."

normal curve (normal distribution)The distribution of probabilities of equally likely events such as the random selection of all possible samples from a population.

open-ended A question or item whose responses are not known ahead of time. Respondents can say or write anything that comes to mind.

open-ends *See*: verbatims.

ordinal level of measurement Two or more response categories in rank order. Using low, medium and high income categories is ordinal.

operationalization (operational definition) Specifications for a variable for how it is to be used in research. It includes all measures, the questions and response categories, check-off lists of behaviors, or other means of observation. It puts a variable into operation with enough specificity that other researchers can replicate it.

p-value The probability that a relation found in a sample is true in the population from which the sample was drawn. Social scientists use a rule of thumb of "$p<.05$," that there is less than a 0.05 chance that the relation is *not* true in the population (0.95 or 95 percent that it *is* true.)

panel study A longitudinal survey using the same sample over the time periods. *See*: longitudinal, cross-sectional, trend and cohort.

parallel form *See*: cross-test reliability.

personal interview (in-person interview) Gathering information face to face.

population A collection of individuals or objects about which information is desired. Also called target, target public, target population or target market.

positive relation Two variables change together such that as one variable's values increase the other's also increase. *See*: relation, negative relation and no relation.

post-test only control group An experiment where observations are made only after the treatment is given.

pretest/post-test control group An experiment where observations are made both before and after the treatment is given.

precision How general or specific an operationalization is. Usually to be more precise is to use more responses in a measure such as using "0 percent to 100 percent" instead of "usually, sometimes, never." *See*: accuracy.

predictive validity How well a variable predicts behavior. *See*: reliability, validity, face validity, content validity, construct validity, internal validity and external validity.

pre-testing Testing items in a scale, a questionnaire, procedures in an experiment and other research material before conducting the actual study.

probability Between zero and one, the likelihood for an event to occur.

probability sample *See*: random sample.

probe A question or instruction designed to follow-up an answer to elicit more depth or breadth of response.

problem statement A written statement of the needs and goals for a potential research project.

qualitative design Formal research using nonsample based designs, usually focusing on words rather than numbers.

quantitative design Formal research using random-sample based designs, usually focusing on numbers rather than words.

quasi-experiment Research that is similar to an experiment but is missing one or more of the elements of an experiment. It does not have random assignment or control of the independent variable or control of external variables.

questionnaire A list of questions, items in a scale and responses.

oversampling Selecting a larger initial sample to account for refusals, no answers and other nonresponse in order to achieve a desired sample size to match an acceptable sampling error.

random The equal chance for all events in a pool of events to happen.

random sample A sample from a population in which each member had an equal chance of being selected. Some techniques for selecting random samples are "simple," "systematic," "stratified," "cluster" and "RDD."

ratio level of measurement Two or more response values with equal intervals, plus the "0" response actually means "none." Most measures involving time or counting, such as hours of TV viewing or age in years, are ratio.

reactive effects People's responses or behaviors are changed because they are sensitized by participating in research.

relation The values of two or more variables change together. *See*: positive relation, negative relation and no relation

relational research (relational analysis) Using two or more variables together to assess the impact of one variable on another. Common relational analyses include: "crosstabulation," "means by subgroups" and "correlation."

reliability Consistency in measures over time and place. Getting a similar answer whether asked inside a building, on the street, this morning or tonight. *See*: validity, internal validity and external validity.

representativeness How well a sample matches a population. Usually tested by computing response rate and comparing known demographics from a census or other studies to the sample's estimates.

research plan A written design of a research project describing each step to be taken, from needs and goals through the final report and presentation.

research question (RQ) Any question containing one or more variables (either descriptive or relational), relating to research needs and goals, that is amenable to research.

respondents Participants in research, usually in a survey.

response rate The proportion or percentage of the sample that participated in the study. This rate does not include sample members that were outside the definition of the population such as businesses in a residential study.

return on investment (ROI) research Research that quantifies the dollar impact of campaigns.

sample A subset of a population, usually random, used to gather information about the population for the purpose of making inferences to the population.

sampling bias *See*: selection bias.

sampling error For numerical estimates from a random sample, the range in which you are confident that the true population value lies.

sampling frame *See*: frame.

scale A series of items or statements with varying response categories that are totaled to get a scale score. Scales usually assess attitudes, opinions and similar variables as opposed to indexes that usually assess how many or how often. *See*: index and precision.

science Observation, description, investigation and theoretical explanation of phenomena. It is empirical, objective, testable and falsifiable.

selection bias The lack of generalizability because people volunteer to participate or a nonrandom sample is used.

self-selection Respondents choose themselves to be in a study.

semantic differential A scale using bi-polar adjectives with an odd number of spaces in between. Respondents check off how close they think a concept is to the adjectives.

significance A statement about the probability of what appears to be a relation between two variables. *See*: statistical test.

significance test *See*: statistical test.

small sample study Research using small groups, usually less than 20.

social science The explanation and prediction of the behavior of human groups.

Solomon four-group An experiment where observations are made both before and after the treatment is given for two groups but only after the same treatment for the other two groups.

stability (test-retest reliability) How consistent responses are from time to time with the same or similar populations.

standard deviation (sd) One standard unit from the center of the normal curve, left or right.

standardization Making sure that questions, stimuli, instructions, procedures and other elements of a study are the same throughout a study in order to be able to replicate any part of the study.

statistical significance *See*: significance.

JOEY REAGAN

statistical test (statistical analysis, statistical inference) A method for assessing the probability that a relation in a sample also exists in the population. Some commonly used tests include chi-square (χ^2), t-test and t-test for Pearson's r.

stimulus The part of an independent variable expected to cause a change in the dependent variable in an experiment.

subjects Participants in research, usually in an experiment.

survey A comprehensive examination of a population, using a random sample, assessing variables for the purposes of describing or finding relations in that population. *See*: longitudinal, cross-sectional, trend, panel and cohort.

syndicated research Research conducted on a regular schedule by companies that store the results and sell them to many clients, such as ratings.

***t*-test for correlations** A significance test where both variables are interval or ratio.

***t*-test for difference of means** A significance test where one variable is nominal with two categories and the other variable is interval or ratio.

target (target public, target population, target market) *See*: population.

telephone technique Gathering information via telephone.

tenacity The basis for explaining how the world works because the explanation has been around a long time or has been often repeated.

test-retest reliability *See*: stability.

theory Based on a body of consistent research, it is a general explanation of behavior from which testable hypotheses can be derived to predict specific behavior.

treatment group *See*: Experimental group.

trend study A longitudinal survey using different samples over the time periods. *See*: longitudinal, cross-sectional, panel and cohort.

validity Whether a measure actually measures what it's supposed to measure. *See*: face validity, predictive validity, content validity, construct validity, internal validity and external validity.

variable Anything that varies or changes such as income, age, or company image. *See*: constant.

variance How much a variable changes when a study is conducted. *See*: explained variance.

verbatim Exact response to open-ended questions.

weighting Balancing data from a sample where important sub-groups are underrepresented, such as having substantially less than 50 percent females in a general population study.

INDEX

confidence interval, 137, 138, 158, 159, 161, 244

confidence level, 137, 138, 158, 216, 244

conjoint analysis, 209

construct validity, 58, 244-247, 250, 253

consultants, 6, 11, 223, 229, 231, 235-239

contact rate, 101, 182

content analysis, 81, 94, 241, 244

content validity, 58, 244-247, 250, 253

controlling the environment, 84

convenience sample, 71, 77, 126, 223

convenience study, 77, 244

cooperation rate, 182

correlation, 61, 62, 67, 68, 126, 181, 189-191, 196, 198, 199, 201, 202, 209, 241, 244

creating new variables, 177

crosstabulation, 181, 189, 196, 201, 202

cross-sectional survey, 71, 92, 95, 221, 223, 245

cross-test reliability, 62, 245, 249

cultural limitations, 107

custom research, 217, 219, 221, 223, 244, 245

D

data analysis, 171, 174, 243

data entry, 169, 171, 173, 174, 177, 243

data file, 113, 131, 171, 174, 178, 179, 213, 236

databases, 7, 105-107, 222

defining the problem, 5, 31

dependent variable, 42, 67, 68, 83, 201, 243, 245, 246, 253

depth interviews, 76, 78, 80, 97, 106, 124, 131, 208, 227, 245

descriptions of the sample, 181

descriptive research, 41, 245

descriptive table, 52, 53

discriminant analysis, 207

distribution, 102, 135, 139, 191, 192, 249

double redundancy, 174

E

effect, 5, 16, 22, 27, 28, 42, 48, 59, 60, 63, 65-69, 75, 83, 84, 86, 87, 89, 92, 95, 115, 199, 201, 203, 239, 243, 245

effect size, 201

elimination of other causes, 68

empiricism, 17

ethics, 2, 6, 14, 27, 168, 229-232

evaluation research, 226, 245

executive summary, 212, 214, 215

experiment, 27, 38, 42, 63, 66, 68, 71, 83-88, 92, 198, 199, 201, 203, 229, 231, 244-247, 249, 250, 252, 253

experimental designs, 85

explained variance, 6, 39, 40, 195, 201, 202, 205, 206, 246, 254

external validity, 62, 244-247, 250, 251, 253

F

face validity, 58, 244, 246, 247, 250, 253

factor analysis, 126, 208

falsifiability (falsifiable), 17, 28, 252

field experiment, 88, 246

focus group, 8, 13, 27, 28, 71, 78-80, 168, 246

focus group agenda, 28, 78

focus group Bill of Rights, 168

formal research, 72, 74, 246, 250

formative research, 226, 246

frame (framing), 29, 109, 116, 147-149, 151-153, 213, 221, 234, 246, 252

frequencies, 186-189, 239, 245

F-test for multiple means, 198, 246

G

goals, 12, 13, 17, 18, 25, 27, 28, 31, 32, 34, 38, 41, 44, 48, 49, 54, 71, 72, 82, 95, 116, 211, 223, 226, 250, 251

H

history of communication research, 5, 19, 21
history of science, 20
history of social science, 20
hypothesis, 12, 42-44, 197, 245-247

I

impact research, 227
in-depth interviews, 76, 78, 80, 97, 106, 124
independent research, 219, 223
independent variable, 42, 67, 68, 83, 84, 243, 245-247, 250, 253
index, 4, 6, 112, 119, 120, 174, 209, 247, 252, 255
inducements, 99
informal research, 7, 72, 247
informed consent, 231
institutional policies, 230
internal communication, 54, 151, 152, 227, 247
internal consistency, 61, 247
internal validity, 59, 61, 85, 244-247, 250, 251, 253
International Association of Business Communicators, 9, 78, 238
Internet tracking, 107
interval, 51-53, 119, 121, 137, 138, 151, 152, 158, 159, 161, 185-187, 189-191, 196-198, 201, 206, 244, 246-248, 253
inter-observer reliability, 61, 247
intuition, 15, 16, 20, 247

in-house research, 223
in-person interview, 97, 98, 249

K

Kadlec Medical Center, 9, 33, 131, 185, 186, 192, 193, 214-216, 224, 225

L

lab experiment, 247
levels of measurement, 51-53, 189, 196, 247
Likert scale, 121, 248
linear regression, 206, 207
longitudinal survey, 92, 94, 244, 248, 249, 253

M

mail technique, 98, 100, 101, 248
mapping, 208, 209
maximum sampling error, 159, 216
mean, 17, 28, 34, 38-40, 47, 49, 58, 60, 67, 93, 109, 115, 137, 141-143, 160, 174, 181, 184, 187, 188, 190-192, 196, 198, 199, 202, 245
means by subgroups, 190, 196, 201, 202
measurement, 17, 49, 51-53, 119-121, 186, 187, 189, 196, 200, 206, 239, 247-249, 251
media monitoring, 227, 248
median, 181, 183, 187, 188, 245
mode, 78, 181, 187, 188, 245
monitoring, 93, 167, 170, 171, 216, 227, 248
multiple response item, 248
multivariate analysis, 6, 126, 203, 205, 206, 248
multi-stage sampling, 221
mutually exclusive, 51, 248

N

needs, 8, 13, 18, 25, 27, 31, 33-35, 38, 41, 44, 47, 48, 63, 65, 71, 72, 82, 92, 94, 107, 113, 116, 159, 162, 173, 184, 205, 211, 212, 215, 223, 226, 227, 246, 250, 251

negative correlation, 191

negative relation, 66, 161, 248, 249, 251

Nielsen Media Research, 9, 213, 219, 220, 239

no relation, 66, 67, 69, 191, 201, 248, 249, 251

nominal, 51-53, 185, 187, 189, 190, 196, 207, 243, 245, 246, 248, 253

nonrandom sample, 157, 248, 249, 252

nonrandom sampling, 71, 155

normal curve, 6, 135-139, 184, 244, 249, 252

O

objectivity, 17

online research, 232

open-ended question (open-ends), 110-112, 131, 173, 177, 249

operationalization, 38, 39, 48-51, 54, 55, 58, 109, 113, 246, 247, 249, 250

oral presentation, 217

ordinal, 51-53, 119, 185, 187-190, 196, 207, 243, 245, 248, 249

other response, 111

oversampling, 162, 250

P

panel study, 92, 249

parallel forms, 62, 245

peer review, 20, 231

personal interview, 60, 97, 171, 247, 249

phone technique, 101, 102

population, 12, 28, 33, 38-41, 60-62, 72, 74, 76, 77, 91-93, 99, 101, 104, 105, 109, 110, 114, 116, 117, 119, 124, 135, 136, 138, 139, 141-144, 147-149, 153-155, 157, 158, 160, 161, 166, 181, 182, 184-186, 195-200, 208, 211, 213, 216, 220, 222, 224, 234, 236, 239, 243-246, 249-254

positive correlation, 190

positive relation, 66, 68, 248, 249, 251

post-test control group, 86, 87, 249

post-test only control group, 249

precision, 52, 63, 123, 234, 241, 243, 250, 252

precision scaling, 123

predictive validity, 58, 244-247, 250, 253

pretest/post-test control group, 86, 249

pretesting, 155, 165, 166, 168, 170, 236

probes, 76, 110, 131, 247

problem statement, 31-34, 37, 42, 50, 77, 250

process research, 227

professionalism, 102, 231, 232

projective techniques, 80

proprietary research, 169

Public Relations Society of America, 12, 237

Q

qualitative designs, 5, 71, 72, 75, 80, 82

qualitative research, 21, 74, 114, 124

quantitative design, 5, 83, 91, 250

quantitative research, 91, 191

quasi-experiment, 85

questionnaire, 12, 28, 29, 38, 50, 55, 60, 74, 84, 85, 97-99, 102-104, 107, 109, 113, 115-118, 130-132, 134, 145, 149, 151, 156, 166-168, 170, 173, 174, 176, 177, 183, 212, 214, 216, 221, 223, 224, 232, 236, 248, 250

R

random digit dialing (RDD), 29, 149, 154, 155, 162, 169, 183, 232

random numbers, 148, 149, 151, 152, 154

random sample, 71, 76, 77, 92, 95, 138, 142, 144, 152, 181, 200, 216, 223, 224, 244, 250, 252, 253

ratio, 51-53, 185, 187, 189-191, 196-198, 201, 206, 216, 244, 246, 248, 251, 253

reactive effects, 62, 251

refusal rate, 182

regression, 59, 60, 206, 207, 241, 248

relational research, 41, 251

relational table, 54

reliability, 5, 8, 57, 61-63, 81, 123, 126, 194, 208, 209, 212, 233, 244-247, 249-253

replication, 42, 44, 58, 109, 161, 224

report method, 216

report table of contents, 214

representativeness, 62, 77, 144, 182, 184, 212, 216, 251

research administration, 6, 165

research plan, 12, 13, 25, 35, 72, 246, 247, 251

research principles, 233, 234

research process, 5, 13, 25, 35, 38, 165

research question, 44, 48, 196, 197, 251

research reports, 6, 7, 17, 191, 211, 213, 231, 233

response rate, 95, 104, 170, 182-184, 216, 251

return on investment, 226, 251

S

sample, 6, 26, 28, 29, 40, 62, 71, 75-77, 92, 93, 95, 107, 117, 118, 124, 126, 135, 136, 138, 141-144, 147-149, 151-163, 168-170, 174, 181-185, 193, 196, 198, 200, 201, 213, 214, 216, 220, 221, 223, 224, 231, 232, 234, 236, 244, 246-254

sample size, 6, 138, 147, 149, 151, 152, 154, 157, 159-163, 216, 236, 248, 250

sampling error, 6, 29, 91, 137, 138, 142, 143, 147, 157-163, 181, 184, 195, 200, 212, 216, 234, 236, 244, 250, 252

SAS, 177, 196

scale, 27, 40, 49, 52, 53, 57, 58, 60-63, 75, 97, 117, 119-126, 129-131, 133, 144, 149, 174, 175, 177, 187, 189, 190, 201, 208, 209, 247, 248, 250, 252

science, 15, 17, 19-21, 23, 28, 74, 135, 158, 195, 229-231, 233, 252

secrecy agreement, 169

selection bias, 59, 60, 64, 104, 153, 251, 252

self-selection, 145, 252

Semantic Differential scale, 122

significance, 6, 68, 136, 137, 142, 185, 195, 196, 198-201, 203, 205, 206, 243, 246, 252, 253

significance test, 196, 198, 243, 246, 252, 253

simple random sampling, 149, 154

small sample study, 118, 252

Solomon four-group, 87

sources of information, 224

split-half reliability, 62

SPSS, 177, 196

stability, 61, 252, 253

standard deviation, 136-138, 252

standardization, 166, 167, 252

stratified sampling, 153

survey, 8, 13, 22, 27, 29, 31, 33, 38, 48, 54, 60, 68, 71, 77, 81, 85, 89, 91, 92, 94, 95, 97, 101, 104, 106, 107, 109, 133, 134, 138, 142, 154, 158, 159, 161-163, 166, 167, 169, 170, 176, 183, 186, 192, 193, 196, 200, 214, 215, 219, 221-224, 227, 229, 231-234, 237, 238, 244, 245, 248, 249, 251, 253

survey designs, 94
syndicated research, 34, 213, 219, 220, 223, 245, 253
systematic random sample, 224
systematically biased, 144

T

target, 8, 15, 18, 34, 38, 44, 48, 50, 53, 63, 65, 72, 74, 81, 104-106, 110, 114, 116, 117, 124, 125, 141, 152, 154, 155, 159, 161, 200, 201, 208, 213, 216, 220-222, 227, 236, 244, 246, 249, 253
telephone interviewer instructions, 167
telephone technique, 253
tenacity, 15, 16, 20, 253
testability, 17
test-retest reliability, 61, 252
time parameter, 49, 55
timeline, 29, 165, 166
time-order, 69, 83
time-series analysis, 208
trend study, 64, 92, 93, 95, 224, 253
t-test, 196-198, 200, 201, 206, 253
t-test for a correlation, 198
t-test for difference of means, 197, 253

U

under-representativeness, 184

V

validity, 5, 8, 27, 57-59, 61-63, 85, 233, 244-247, 250, 251, 253
variable(s), 5, 8, 25, 27, 28, 34, 35, 37-45, 47-54, 57-59, 61, 63, 65-69, 75, 83, 84, 89, 92, 95, 107, 109, 119, 121, 124, 130-133, 141, 166, 174, 175, 177, 181, 184-191, 195-198, 201-203, 205-208, 226, 236, 243- 253, 254
variable name, 175
variance, 5, 6, 37, 39, 40, 195, 201, 202, 205, 206, 246, 254
verbatim(s), 96, 111, 117, 131, 173, 174, 192, 193, 213, 239, 249, 254
verification, 15, 167, 171, 174, 176, 216, 236
volunteers, 34, 145, 157

W

weighting, 184, 185, 234, 254
World Advertising Research Center, 239

Z

zero correlation, 191